Queen's Applause...

"From the title and throughout every page, this book spoke to my spirit for I too was a young girl who felt the stigma of the negative things that society delivered to those whom I resembled. I can recall countless times when I felt less than and in need of some guidance in finding my true, authentic self. I needed to find a way to realize my self-worth. Times have changed dramatically which makes this manifesto even more important.

The breaking down of households, historical facts, the different areas of a young woman's life that are paramount for a positively productive life are deeply discussed which helps to further engrain the understanding of who we are, why we are and who we are destined and able to become. Labeling sections "Apps" is an ingenious way of connecting the text to current "lingo" and it helps to make it applicable to the generation of today.

This book is a MUST read! Dr. Rouse has done it again! She is an incredible role model for showing young women that there's more to being a woman than just incredible beauty; she not only has that in great abundance, but she also has brains, passion, tenacity and power to make a difference. Dr. Rouse is what is needed today for our young African–American Queens."

Dr. Samone M. Smith-Brown

Permit Psychologist, Certified Life Coach, Motivational Speaker

"An amazing compilation of practical topics that many African American girls may encounter as they navigate issues related to social/emotional and academic development. Dr. Rouse's strategy of untangling these issues through the use of an understanding coach-tone approach has made this book a 'must have' for young girls. "

Edris Ryan, Ph.D.

"Born a Queen Indeed! What an inspiring, multifaceted self-discovery 'journal'. Dr. Angelise Rouse is a compassionate educator who loves children and inspires them to be the Kings and Queens they were created to be. Kudos Angelise...I'm excited to see what is next. Continue to Live Your Purpose, Continue to Inspire young people of color. Thank you for walking out your greatness so our people will have positive, educated people of color with integrity to model. Shine like a Flawless diamond!"

Shirreca Bradham, Educator

"This book is important! The information is imperative to the success of African-American young women. From education, to family, to morals and more, this book hits every point in detail and leaves no stone unturned. Oftentimes, we as woman are thrown into life without direction and expected to sink or swim. It's refreshing to have a guide to help along the way."

Lashae Latimore, Author and Owner of Love and Literature Publications

BORN A
QUEEN

Practical Advice for Young African-American Females

Dr. Angelise M. Rouse

Printed in the United States of America

2018 First Edition

Subject Index:

Rouse, Angelise M.

Title: Born A Queen:

Practical Advice for Young African-American Females

1. Black 2. Youth 3. Empowerment 4. Inspirational 5. Self-Help

Paperback ISBN: 978-0-9976546-3-9

Ebook ISBN: 978-0-9976546-2-2

Library of Congress Control Number: 2018911887

Especially 4 Me Publishing LLC

especially4mepublishing.com

drangeliserouse.com

www.especially4mepublishing.com

This book is dedicated to my daughter,

Alyse Marie Rouse

A MESSAGE TO YOUNG FEMALES...

Who run the world? Girls!
Who run the world? Girls!

— Beyoncé

Let's Get It! Lace up your favorite kicks or slip into your designer shoe and get moving! There's no time like the present to take your rightful place in society. You are a queen. All of the women in your lineage stem from royalty. Don't settle for mediocrity. Use your mind and God-given talents to be the best *you* that you can be. Work with what you have. Run with skill, grace and intention. The world is waiting on you to own your innate position and be great!

Go! See! Learn! Conquer!

CONTENTS

CONTENTS

"Black Girls... Don't be afraid to use your voice. Your thoughts, opinions, and ideas are just as important as anybody else's. When you speak, speak with boldness and purpose. Have courage, be confident, and always be true to yourself! Live your life fearlessly! Your voice has GREAT power; don't be afraid to utilize it when needed. You're NOT an angry Black woman; you're a woman who has something important to say. Your voice matters and so do YOU."

–Stephanie Lahart

ROYAL GOALS

You should have a journal where you write down ideas, thoughts and your daily encounters. Why not purchase another type of notebook where you begin to write out your "Royal Goals?" In your new book, use the first few pages to jot down all of the things that you like to do, the things that you are good at, and what your ideal Plan A is for your career. Then research several types of schools in your area to decide if you want to stay home and commute, attend online, or go out-of-state. You'd be surprised at the hundreds of majors and career opportunities that exist for nearly anything you can think of. Are you great with numbers or computers? Are you good at writing and communicating? Do you have a gift to draw, act, or design products?

Again, do your research. Find people who are operating in a field that you think you want to go into. Contact the school's counseling department to talk with a career professional. Nothing can supplement an educated mind which will give you a foundation to build upon and an opportunity to be the best version of yourself. As you are getting closer to finalizing your Plan A, then begin working on Plan B. The more you plan and prepare to succeed, the better your chances of actual success.

INTRODUCTION

#Walkinitnow

"When I dare to be powerful - to use my strength in the service of my vision, then it becomes less and less important whether I am afraid."

— Audre Lorde

After publishing **The King Inside: Practical Advice for Young African-American Males**, I received an overwhelmingly positive response. I knew that it would only be a short time before I wrote a similar book to equip and empower my young African-American sisters.

As an educator, I specifically wanted to write a book for young women because I see so many beautiful girls who don't appreciate their special and unique qualities. It's all too easy to see what's beautiful in other people, but in ourselves, we often manage to only see what we don't like.

In spite of the negative stories and viral images attempting to degrade your character, I challenge you to focus on the inside and the rich cultural history that destined you for greatness. Black women are charting new courses in key career fields, whether STEM, business, medicine, education, entertainment, fashion, politics and social responsibility. Our numbers are rising and our network is stronger than ever before. With your commitment to advancing yourself in education, spirituality and self-care, there is no limit to what we can achieve as a collective group and be an unstoppable force.

In **Born A Queen**, I have provided key principles for you to reflect upon as you mature into womanhood. Every "App" is designed for you to take inventory of where you are at this important stage in your life. Of course there is no one-size fits all girl-power growth lesson, but I believe there is something here for everyone: family, money, business, relationships and more. If there's one thing that I want every young lady to take from this book is the ability to grow, discover and celebrate her own unique self. After all, before you were born, God knew you and blessed your birthright. It's yours to possess. So just run with it, because there's nothing anyone can do to take away from the fact that you, my love, were **Born A Queen**!

Dr. Angelise M. Rouse
October 2018
Burlington, New Jersey

APP # 1
FAMILY FOUNDATION
#Iamthefamilyoaktree

"You don't choose your family. They are God's gift to you as you are to them."

— Bishop Desmond Tutu

For many of you reading this book, this will be the chapter to help you better understand who you are and why you do things a certain way. Your family is where you learn everything about life. It is your interconnection with family which creates your values, self-esteem, work ethic, mental health and general view of life.

The Black family in America is an unique structure in the community. The horrific events of slavery and the historical separation of the Black family continues to affect the family unit today. During those times, it was against the law for Blacks to be educated. Therefore, high illiteracy passed from generation to generation. Black women had to take on larger roles in the family and were subject to rape and other abuses from their White slave owners.

Today, the Black family has been shaped by years of misconceptions, racism, economic struggles, and the strength of the Black woman. There is so much media misrepresentation about the Black family that the masses can only feed into the negativity, and not see the bigger, more beautiful picture. Granted, there are challenges in the Black family, but there are challenges in *all* families regardless of race, ethnicity and culture. To properly tackle the Black family issue, I will divide it into four subheadings: (i) two parent household, (ii) single parent household; (iii) foster household and (iv) blended families.

The Two-Parent Household

If you grew up in a family with both parents still together and living in the same household, then you are amongst the fortunate girls in America. This is true not just for Black women, but for all races. Divorce rates and single parenthood are so prevalent that it has become almost abnormal to have both parents in your household to guide you through life. Living in a two-parent household today is a real privilege. Does this mean that all of your problems are automatically solved? Of course not! You may have the parental guidance and supervision you need, but you could misuse it or take it for granted, if you are not careful.

> *"Be thankful for what you have; you'll end up having more. If you concentrate on what you don't have, you will never, ever have enough."*
>
> **— Oprah Winfrey**

With so many technological distractions including cell phones, video games and social media, young people do not realize the value of their parents' input to help them avoid mistakes in life. Let's face it, if your parents can't talk to you, then who can? Yes, some parents abuse their children because of many different reasons. They may suffer from anxiety or depression disorder, mental illnesses, alcohol and drug dependences, or have been a victim of abuse themselves. But the majority of parents want to see their children succeed and avoid the mistakes that they made when they were younger, or help steer you in the right direction from making bad decisions.

As an African-American young lady, growing up, especially in the inner cities, your parents will take extra steps to protect you. They have been there, they know the dangers and cannot imagine you being in the same situation. Don't take your parent's presence for granted. Listen and learn from them. To paraphrase Oprah's quote, "if you focus on what your family lacks, you will never find happiness in reality."

Right now, your father may be tough on you. There is a valid reason. It does not mean that he hates you and doesn't want to see you happy. The need for a good relationship between a girl and her father is not usually talked about in the Black community. Yet, you need your daddy's guidance. He is more than likely, the first man you will ever know and love. He will teach you how to be loved, protected and respected by a man. You should not be afraid of your father, instead, respect him and listen to his advice about boys and men. There is no better person to advise you on the subject of boys than your dad.

Understand that your mom and dad are separate beings and have different emotions and feelings. If you think your parents don't get you, build the courage to talk to them. In a family, communication is the key to understanding each other. Just because they are your parents, doesn't mean they know everything that is going on in your mind. Whether you like it or not, genetically, many characteristics of both of your parents are in you, so focus on demonstrating the good and work on changing the bad.

Speak up about your feelings girl! Be bold enough to confide in the people who love you. Don't think outsiders are more important than your family. It's OK to be a little frustrated by the behaviors of your parents or siblings. It's normal. There is no perfect family anywhere in the world - not even the Royal Family. If you have siblings, learn to get along with them. Even though they may annoy you sometimes, your best strategy is to observe and understand the personality of your siblings so that you can help and encourage one another. When you get older, you will appreciate each other a lot more.

Try to establish a strong bond with family members even if you find it challenging. Black girls growing up in a two parent household already have what many girls dream of. Make sure you talk things out with your parents and siblings.

To be clear, I am not saying if there are toxic, abusive people in your family that you should embrace them. Whether the abuse is physical, mental or emotional, it is better to keep your space and love them from a distance. Sharing the same family bloodline does not mean that everyone gets along all the time. Disagreements are a part of family life. Many things can lead to conflict such as sickness, disability, addiction, job loss, school problems, and marital issues. Listening to each other and working to resolve conflicts are important in strengthening the family.

Remember, you did not choose your family. They were chosen before you were born. None of us have any say in the matter. Establishing open communication within your family is important, but sometimes talking to your family may be too problematic. Some family issues can sometimes put you in a very upsetting or even unsafe situation. Talk to a grown up you trust like a teacher, mentor, friend's parent or school counselor about your family issues to get help or see things from a different perspective.

The Single-Parent Household

At 77%, African-American households have the highest percentage of children born to unmarried mothers. This rate is indeed alarming, while the national non-immigrant average is 42%, and it was 30% for whites as reported by The National Center for Health Statistics in 2015.

Despite this, single mothers have been the backbone of the Black community. They have gone out of their way to ensure that their kids have all they need to succeed in life.

I'm not putting the blame on anyone. If this is your reality, learn to appreciate the efforts of your hardworking mother, instead of focusing on what you don't have. We all need to feel loved and appreciated. Unfortunately, many young girls brought up by single mothers under appreciate the love of their mothers.

Research has shown the negative effects of children growing up in single-parent households contributes to children being more aggressive, rebellious, high school dropouts, abuse drugs and alcohol, struggle with mental health, and fall into poverty. More disturbing results suggest that girls may be prone to sexually promiscuous behavior, which thus spikes the teenage pregnancy rate in the U.S. (Black Los Angeles, 2011).

If you are from a single parent home, don't buy into the negative statistics of your future. Instead, it should be your wake up call to want more, do more and be better.

> *"Mistakes are a fact of life. It is the*
> *response to the error that counts."*
>
> **— Nikki Giovanni**

Whatever happened between your parents is not your fault. Life can be challenging. Sometimes you'll find yourself in less than ideal situations. Society puts more pressure on women to meet high, often unattainable standards. It's your fault if you choose to let your circumstances determine your future. Your mom may not have the quality time for you right now because she is busy playing several roles.

As a teacher, I see a lot of girls with low self-esteem. I know it's inevitable to sometimes avoid feeling deprived of love in a single parent household. There are millions of kids that may be worse off than you. Even in homes where both parents are present, children still get abused, violated and neglected. So, if you have *one* loving parent, it's more than enough. Your focus should be on building your life instead of searching for what could have or would have been.

It's normal if you feel the need for a man's attention. Just be selective in your decision-making because your worth is not measured in the arms of a man. If you feel you are not getting enough love at home, I assure you that the love, respect and acceptance you long for is not in the streets. You can find fulfillment in working with support groups and your local church. When you need to confide in someone other than your mom, talk to a counselor at school or church. The best gift you can give to your own kids is becoming the best version of yourself. Start now. Aim to create meaning in your life and turn the negative numbers of being a product of a single mom into positive ones.

> *"Be the change that you*
> *wish to see in the world."*
>
> **— Mahatma Gandhi**

The high level of single mom's in Black American society is a learned behavior caused by inescapable environmental factors. Many of the men in the community expose the single mom and child to negative lifestyles by being affiliated with gangs and violence, incarceration, domestic abuse, lack of education, unemployment and abuse of drugs and alcohol. If you are serious about changing your life and you are involved with a guy engaging in any of these activities, it's time to change your situation. Don't allow the negative stereotype to be the ending narrative of your story. You can be the change. You can break the generational cycle and make Gandhi's famous quote personal: "*I am the change I want to see in myself.*"

The greatest love of all is learning to love yourself. Make the choice to let the negative feelings and situations inspire you to press harder each day. Let the love of your mother be enough to propel you forward. Be strong, yet seek help when you need it. There is a saying that I often quote to my children, " You can choose to react negatively to your circumstances and be in bondage or have freedom and take control of your life with a positive reaction."

Being the child of a single mother is not an automatic cause for failure in life. I am not ignoring the fact that you may struggle sometimes, but there is always a different way to look at your situation and change your perspective. You will pull through the tough times if you are deliberate and proactive. You are valuable. You are worthy. Do not let your background define your destiny. You and your single mother are royalty.

> *"My mama was single and raised me…*
> *she is all the reason I am who I am!!"*
>
> **— Alicia Keys**

The Foster Household

> *"Family is supposed to be our*
> *safe haven. Very often, it's the place*
> *where we find the deepest heartache."*
>
> **— Iyanla Vanzant**

The separation of the Black family and the challenges our communities face in creating productive citizens has had a rippling effect on our children. Black children are being raised outside of their biological families. While some children are placed with caring foster parents, others are not so fortunate, given the broken state of many of America's child welfare systems. Many children are simply shifted from one toxic home to another.

This should be disturbing for anyone, but considering that African-American children make up a sizeable percentage of children in foster care, the effects of a broken child welfare system impacts the African-American community even more severely (Burdick, L. 2016).

According to The Adoption and Foster Care Analysis and Reporting System 2016, two out of ten children in foster care are African-Americans. Black children, especially those from low-income backgrounds, are separated from their biological families at higher rates than other races. However, according to the same study, trends reveal that the percentage of Black children in care decreased between 2006 and 2016, while the percentages of White children, Hispanic children, and children of other races or multiracial children increased.

My advice to you is to do your best and focus on school, be patient, be determined to succeed, and you will have a greater chance to reach your goals.

Always continue to work on yourself because being in foster care is just one phase of your life. Upon turning 18 or earlier, your parents may be more stable or better yet, you will finally have the chance to live on your own. Until that time, work on yourself without being distracted from the negative thoughts that may hinder you. For those of you in foster care with good foster parents, listen to them, respect them and reciprocate their love. Let them know that they made a good decision by giving you an opportunity to succeed in life.

However, if you are placed in an unfavorable home, remind yourself daily that this is just a temporary phase. Avoid taking out your frustrations on your foster parents or others around you. Do your best to be considerate as you figure out how to occupy your time constructively. I know that being in the system is an emotional rollercoaster, but don't let your emotions control you because you have more important things to do in the future.

Family Patterns

A mistake by your family member is not *your* mistake. Break the cycle and be the one that changes the narrative. If your family is experiencing adversities, use this as your inspiration to be the change you want. Negative or positive, your family history is where you need to look in order to understand your life and the struggles you are facing. However, as I mentioned earlier, it's totally up to you to be the change you want to see.

Families are not only good when they are doing positive things. Their negative behaviors can also help us avoid pitfalls in life. For example, if everyone in your family is struggling financially, use this experience to prompt you to begin learning money management skills.

Look at the patterns of occurrences in your family and decide how they are affecting you. Granted, the negative generational behaviors exist, whether it be poverty, debt, domestic violence, emotional abuse, single parenthood, incarceration or drug abuse. Yet, it could also be positive like a college education or good work ethic. Now is the time to begin to lay the necessary foundation needed to help you create a stable and positive, functional home for your own family.

Take your time and write down your family traits that you notice, and use it as a guide. Make a pledge to follow the positive path and actions and seek help to avoid the negatives.

> *"Don't wait around for other people to be happy for you. Any happiness you get you've got to make yourself."*
>
> — *Alice Walker*

It's unwise to keep repeating the same behaviors hoping that things will magically turn around. Make a conscious effort to avoid negative patterns in your family. You do not have to do it alone, sure it will be hard, yet reach out to someone or support groups. You'll be surprised that there are people willing to help you break free; many of whom were in the same or similar situation as yourself. If you are being emotionally or sexually abused, then call the child care help hotline immediately. Your goal is to be included in the positive statistics. Break the cycle of negativity, lack and despair as you remain focused. Soar above your struggles.

Blended Families

For a number of reasons, being connected to a blended family has become the norm. Having a stepmother or stepfather and step siblings can be an added bonus to your growth and maturity. Blended families can be stressful for both the parents and children, but it takes real effort and patience. Like any personal relationship, there needs to be a mutual respect for each other. There may also be a need for adjustments to be made as it relates to the rules of your old house versus your new house. Learning to adapt to new environments and being civil to others will help you to become a better person as a daughter or sister.

Mirror, Mirror

Queen Michelle Obama:
Ancestry Revealed

The historical significance of President Barack Obama's eleva-
tion to the White House in 2009 is something that anyone who
witnessed it will never forget. For the first time in American History, an African-American held the highest office in the country.
The Obama family were a beacon of hope for African-Americans that if you work hard, you can achieve your dreams.

The world became privy to the love, respect, admiration and
educational accomplishments of the Black family as a solid
unit. You could see the love Barack has for his wife Michelle
and their two daughters. You felt the love Michelle has for her
husband, her mother and her daughters. This was the first time
that a mother-in-law resided in the White House. The Obama's
showed the world that family is everything.

As First Lady, many articles were written about Michelle Obama's past. A genealogist from *The New York Times* traced Mrs. Obama's ancestry to her great-great-great-grandmother, an enslaved girl named Melvinia. In 1850, Melvinia's owner in South Carolina divided up his assets in his will and she was valued at $475 at the age of eight. Melvinia was sent to Alabama and became impregnated by a white man around the age of 15. The specific portions of Michelle Obama's ancestry revealed that her family roots began in South Carolina, rural Georgia, Alabama, Chicago and then the White House.

Since you don't get to choose your family, it is important to know your history and honor the sacrifices of your ancestors. There are several genealogy companies offering to help you fill in your historical gaps. Research them to see which one best fits your needs.

Queen's Wisdom

"No matter what accomplishments you make, somebody helped you. "

— *Althea Gibson*

We were all created to be in relationship with one another. Good health, happiness and success does not come to those who operate alone. Spend time talking to your parents, grandparents, aunts, uncles, and extended relatives to gain insight into who they are and how they became the person they are today. Learn from their mistakes and successes. Have family meetings where everyone feels welcome to share thoughts, challenges and wisdom, all rooted in love.

★ Every member of your family is a human being. Humans are flawed. It's OK to not get along with a family member. Learn to love those that are hard to love from a distance.

★ Don't think that you are the smartest person in your family. There is something to learn from each generation. Lean in and gain valuable insight to life.

★ Plan regular family outings to do things as a group or in the community. Changing the environment by working together as a team to accomplish a specific goal will build strong relationships.

★ Try to avoid the family cliques and gossip train about other family members. Rumors can hurt and may create unnecessary long-term division for generations.

You are a branch on your family tree. Your legacy starts with you. You can change the trajectory of your family history and future just like Michelle Obama. #Iamthefamilyoaktree.

APP#2
Educational Foundation

#Throwyourcapintheair

*"Education is everything–education
is your power, your way in life
for whatever you want to do."*

— Ciara

Although I am not surprised, it was refreshing to read a study by the National Center for Education Studies, which found that Black women had the highest percentage of college enrollment than any other group in America. Congratulations! Wave your hands and caps in the air! This means we must be doing something right, but we could do more.

The majority of the discussions about the struggles of the Black community center around the need for advanced education. Yet most times, the focus is on helping African-American young men, while African-American young women are left to figure it out on their own.

Fortunately, as this study demonstrates, many African-American women have refused to settle for stereotypical roles in their homes and in the service industries. We have taken control of our lives by achieving higher education degrees.

The great thing about earning advanced degrees today is that there are more options than ever before. Not to mention the added benefits of the convenience of earning your degree online. There really is no excuse anymore if you desire a better life and career options. I know you can do this. The writing is already on the wall. Of course, knowledge won't totally eliminate your struggles or life's challenges. Yet the more knowledge you acquire, the more likely your perspective of the challenge will shift and help you overcome it in a manner that would not have been possible without an education.

I am not saying obtaining a college degree and higher is all you need to succeed in life, but a degree or certification with a marketable skill is essential to have more options. So many people confuse literacy, the ability to read and write, with a proper education. It's not the same thing.

Education broadens the horizons of your mind. There is credible research which shows that with a higher educational background, you are able to make a better decision than someone who graduated high school. Think about it. How can you enlarge your views if you and your friends come from similar or the same backgrounds, live in the same community, shop and eat at the same places, watch the same TV programs, and work in the same retail or the fast food industry? Do you realize that all of your actions and thoughts are based on a narrow viewpoint of your *own* limited, yet comfortable world? There is so much more happening around you here in the United States and around the globe in business, economics, politics and social responsibility, that you have no idea about, yet these issues can have a direct impact on your future.

> *"The roots of education are*
> *bitter, but the fruit is sweet."*
> — **Aristotle**

There is no question that education gives you an edge in life. Our ancestors fought so we could have the opportunity to better our lives. We are standing on their shoulders when we use our minds to help make changes in society. As young African-American women, your needs have often been neglected especially, if you are from a less privileged background. In spite of the systematic failures in the American educational system, acquiring an education is one of the best ways to get out of poverty, uplift yourself emotionally and gain financial freedom.

> *"Through my education, I didn't just*
> *develop skills, I didn't just develop*
> *the ability to learn, but I developed*
> *confidence."*
> **— Michelle Obama**

I realize that there are a lot of celebrities and business leaders who became successful without getting an education, but most of them also had luck on their side. Comparing yourself to celebrities is unrealistic because only a small percentage of the population will become rich and famous.

I want you to disregard what the media is telling you that some of the most successful people in the world are not educated - this narrative is flawed, and the uneducated success stories in business are few and far between. Mark Zuckerberg would not have met the people that helped him build Facebook if he was not enrolled at Harvard. The same goes for the late Steve Jobs, who used the typeface for the first Mac computer from what he learned in a calligraphy class in college. In life, being at the right place at the right time is an important part of success. College is where you will meet great minds aspiring to build a brighter future for themselves. You won't be limited by your background when you go to college because the experience provides plenty of opportunities to lift yourself beyond your situation.

There's not many success stories for low-skilled workers. Going to school might be difficult for you right now and you may even feel like the teacher does not get you. The teacher's role is to help you move to the next level. It's your job to put forth a genuine effort to show that you earned your right to be there.

Many African-American girls that I teach are forced to deal with responsibilities earlier in life than they are supposed to, which can weigh heavily on them emotionally. Such stress has caused them to lose focus, become argumentative and give up on striving for better opportunities. Don't give in to the pressure and don't give up on your Plan A for self-improvement.

Taking Care of Business

Being in a multicultural educational environment will better prepare you to handle people and understand humanity. Although, I know in some classrooms, Black girls are often viewed as bringing less value to the discussion table, impact your class in the beginning and show your brilliance. Bring your thoughts and opinions to the conversation with confidence. Know your worth. You're not there to impress others with your clothes or hairstyles. You are in an educational environment to learn, to discover your true self and to learn how to be comfortable in your own skin. Be prepared and accept the fact that some days in the classroom will be tougher than others, but when you focus on the *why* rather than the difficulties, you'll find the strength to persevere and finish what you started.

Realistically, no matter what you want to do in today's advanced tech world, you still need to have critical thinking skills to help you solve problems for many different types of organizations.

By furthering your education, you won't just learn facts, you will be exposed to a different environment of peers from various cultures, ethnicities, and religions, that will allow you to build your social skills, learn time management, and understand the ideologies that shape the world.

Whether we like it or not, Artificial Intelligence (AI) has become a norm in our society. What would we do without our cell phones and all of its seamless connections to our daily lives? Only those with advanced degrees will have a chance at obtaining these high in-demand careers. Now that we have become accustomed to the benefits of 4G technology, all the buzz is for the world to get ready for 5G technology, which may be thousands of times faster than 4G. Do we really need to watch a show or ask Google a question at lightning speed? I don't believe so. However, the key for you to take away from this chapter is that everything as we know it is moving faster and faster, and if you don't have a plan to inject yourself into the fold, you will be quickly left behind. Whether it's getting a well-paying job or building a reputable business, without an education that gives you a needed economic skill set, your life will be more challenging.

The reason I keep encouraging young Black girls to focus on maintaining a strong academic background is because there is enough evidence to point to the fact that the future will be run by machines. The factory jobs are not coming back, neither is the need for low-skilled labor. According to international statistics, AI will eliminate 40% of the current jobs in the U.S. alone, while the population will continue to grow. You need to make a serious decision today to prepare yourself if you want to escape poverty in the future because the gap between "the have's" and "the have not's" will only get wider.

I am not trying to scare you, but it's the truth. To make things worse, people who can't make good decisions will be at the mercy of those who can. Check your social media feeds and see how many people are trying to sell their products and ideas to you. If you cannot think critically, then you're 10 times more likely to make impulsive decisions. If you are already a shopper, you are falling into the trap. Do you want to be at the mercy of others forever or take control of your life today?

Life is not fair. Life does not bow to one person's wish. You need to be prepared to take your life into your hands. It's never going to be easy. In fact, one of the worst things you can do is convince yourself that things are going to get easier. Nothing worth achieving ever comes easy. Yes, your needs aren't being met by the failing American educational system. Yes, you are being shunned by society. But, their opinions will not determine who you were birthed to be. The only way you can become your best self is by expanding the limitations of your mind through education.

> *"Education is the most powerful weapon*
> *which you can use to change the world."*
> — ***Nelson Mandela.***

Michelle would not have met Barack if they both had not graduated from college and worked at the same law firm. Their education allowed them to achieve a level of success and make a social impact that they never dreamed possible. You too can use education to not only change your life, but to change the world. You could create businesses that help make the lives of millions of people better and encourage other Black girls to follow your path of success and positivity.

The former president of Harvard, Derek Bok once said, "If you think education is expensive, try ignorance." Taking out a loan to attend college is a good strategy as long as you know that you'll graduate. The key is finishing with a skill that is in demand. As long as you choose to take out a loan, I encourage you to study a science degree like engineering, medicine, nursing, finance or other high-demand careers because they generally pay more after graduating college and can help you pay back your loans sooner.

I am not saying that you can't follow your passion in life. You just have to understand that supply and demand is the basis of economics. There was a time when coal miners and factory workers were in demand. Now it's all about tech, business and health. Your life's purpose is not just about how you feel because most times our emotions lead us down the wrong path. You can always use your artistic creativity as a side hustle or even change careers in the future. Any degree that won't help you pay off your student loans within a few years after graduation should be reconsidered.

You are multitalented. A degree is supposed to prepare you for the future. You don't want to go back into the struggle after graduation. Do your research, be wise and make an economic decision to major in a career that will set you on the path of financial freedom.

> *"You're not obligated to win. You're obligated to keep trying to do the best you can every day."*
>
> **— Marian Wright Edelman**

Mirror, Mirror

Queen Lauren Simmons:
The Only African-American Female Stockbroker
on The New York Stock Exchange

I think it's important to recognize that we all have many gifts and talents. Once you decide to further your education to acquire an undergraduate degree, masters, or Ph.D., you may come to realize that the career that you have been working towards for your major, may not be where you start out or end up.

A great example of this is Lauren Simmons. She can actually be mistaken for one of the daughters of Rev. Run on *Growing Up Hip Hop*, based on her features and her last name. However, there appears to be no relation. Ms. Simmons is currently the only African-American female stockbroker on the New York Stock Exchange, at only 23 years old. She is an equity trader for Rosenblatt Securities.

With a B.A. degree in genetics and a minor in statistics, she envisioned her career in the medical field, but worked on an internship for clinical trials and realized that medicine was not for her. As fate would have it, she always had a love for numbers and moved to New York from Georgia, and applied for positions in finance. She was fortunate to respond to a position on LinkedIn.

To secure her full-time role, Ms. Simmons had one month to pass the Series 19 Exam, which is rooted in financial principles and concepts. She studied hard and passed the first time. Many people doubted her, and now that she is the only female in a sea of white males, she has proven the doubters wrong. Lauren stated,

"When I see statistics that say '80 percent don't get through,' I look at the 20 percent." So when everyone kept saying, 'It's a hard test. Don't worry if you don't pass,' for me, I needed to pass to prove to myself that I could do this."

Queen's Wisdom

"I wish I had known that education is the key.
That knowledge is power."
— Mary J. Blige

No matter how book smart you are or how smart you think you are, trust me, neither you nor anyone else knows everything about life. It's impossible. Even Plato, considered one of the smartest men who ever lived, admitted that *he* knew nothing. The best thing that will help you in today's technological world is to open your mind to learning new things and learning from others.

Now that you are on a royal journey, don't look at where you are right now as your final destination. Life is all about the moments. There will be times when you feel like the world is against you and times when you'll on top of the world. The school phase does not last forever. You don't have to like your peers, the food or the professors. All that matters is that you get what you signed up for: a degree or credentials that will help you move further in life.

An educational environment can be fun. Your experience is what you make it. It can be a beautiful moment, so enjoy it while it lasts. As you are studying and taking the next phase of your life seriously, consider these Queen's Wisdom points to help guide you.

★ Be the boss of your feelings. Don't let your emotions or feelings control you.

★ You don't have to be the smartest in the room, just show up and do your best.

★ Don't avoid the competition at school. The world is full of competition. Learn from it. Use your gifts to your advantage. Strive to win.

★ Don't spend your day complaining about your life. You must adapt and learn from your situations. The goal is to grow a little stronger and wiser each day.

★ Teachers and professors are there to help you, but they are human. In my environments, Black girls have a reputation for talking back to their teachers and disrespecting authority. Hold your tongue. Check your attitude. Being young does not mean it's impossible to sit yourself down and reflect on your actions. This is what makes us human. Consider how your behavior affects others and the impact it might have on you in the future.

★ If you are struggling with life decisions, then talk to an adult. If there's no one at home to help, talk to a teacher or a counselor at school. If you feel no one understands you, then pick up the phone and call a support line.

You're a queen in the making. There are people who see your potential and are willing to help you if you ask. Don't shut the world out. Approach your educational pursuit with diligence, commitment and intentionality. This is your opportunity to become the best version of yourself. #Throwyourcapintheair!

APP# 3
SPIRITUALITY FOUNDATION

#Dailyspiritualitycheckup

"There's nothing wrong with not having figured out who you are, but so much can go wrong when you pretend that you have."

— Sarah Jakes Roberts

A s a young female, you probably have not given much thought about your spirituality unless you regularly attend a church, temple, mosque or other place of worship. Spirituality in a general sense is realizing that we are connected to something much bigger than ourselves. It is an experience that everyone can relate to when we tap into that inner voice that provides comfort, peace and direction.

Many find it through prayer. Others find it through meditation, in nature or a physical activity. The main takeaway is that when you connect with your spirituality, you should have a better understanding of who you are.

Keep in mind that religion and spirituality are not the same thing. Even though spirituality may have some elements of religion tied to it, they are not the same. Religion often times is based on a written doctrine that helps you determine right and wrong. Spirituality, on the other hand, helps you personally find the meaning of life. It is also connected to your emotional health and well-being, and is based on the premise of being in a positive state of mind to allow you to see things clearer or from another perspective.

You can find a sense of spirituality listening to relaxing music or reading inspirational books. Basically, anything that touches you on the inside and makes you feel a sense of peace during or right after the moment, can be considered spiritual. Your interactions and connections with others can also be spiritual.

I certainly cannot speak for everyone, but my spirituality gives me a sense of purpose and direction for my life. It is important for you to find your spiritual foundation as well. I believe my personal growth and connection to others is a result of my spirituality. It keeps me grounded and reminds me that "it's not all about me" and that I am here to somehow help others, which is something that truly makes me feel fulfilled. That is why I chose a career in teaching. The idea of giving back and helping young people achieve their dreams is my driving force.

I think spirituality is difficult to put in words because it is a feeling. However, like anything worth doing, it takes some type of intentional action to get better at it and to be focused. The more you step away from the noise to find a quiet place and really pay attention to your environment by taking in the sights, sounds and smells around you, the more mindful you will become of the beautiful things in Creation. Each day dedicate a few minutes of quiet time to take in your surroundings and enjoy the moment.

What's Your Moral Compass?

The term "moral compass" refers to your decision-making in determining right from wrong. It is your inner voice that guides you. Hopefully, you have developed a moral compass to do the right thing. By now, you should have a clear sense as to what is right and what is wrong.

As you will see, life is all about the personal decisions you make. The more good decisions you act upon, the better your chances of success. On the flip side, the more bad decisions you engage in, the fewer opportunities you will have for your future. So when your girls decide that they want to shoplift from the local mall, your decision to engage in this type of activity is a bad decision. If you go through with it and don't get caught the first time, the sheer excitement and rush will convince you to do it again. But you shouldn't. It's highly likely, that this second time, you will get caught and end up in jail.

Engaging in any type of illegal activity is ultimately the wrong decision. The more times you get away with something, the harder it will be for you to stop. It becomes a bad habit that feels too good to break. The key is to not get involved in the first place.

Having a good moral compass is the only way to survive in life. The temptation to do wrong is so easy and it is everywhere. Corruption is rampant in politics, business, school systems, and even religious institutions. Money and greed will continue to be the downfall of people. You are stronger than you think. Resist the temptation to do wrong and tap into your moral compass as often as possible.

Mind & Body

Meditation

The more time you spend observing and relaxing in your environment, the easier it will be for you to begin the practice of meditation. I have read that there is actually scientific evidence to show how your brain changes the longer you meditate. There is a great deal of information to verify that being still every day for at least 15-30 minutes can make a big difference in how things affect you and your interaction with others.

Meditation helps you to become calm about things that the average person who does not meditate may find offensive or angered. Practicing it daily will literally shift your focus from yourself and give you a desire to connect and help others. I think researching how meditation can change your brain for the better is definitely something worth looking into. Spirituality and meditation deal with your mind, so learning about both will give you an advantage. Yet in order to be effective in your daily life and personal growth, you must not only work on improving your mind, but also your body.

Stay Pure

Clean living is vital. From the food you eat to the water you drink, it is important that you try to keep your body pure so you can stay healthy, active and energetic. Still, it is tough to totally keep your body free of toxins. Just walking down the street, you are breathing in environmental pollutants. Plus, we're constantly in contact with different chemicals in our food, beauty products and cleaning supplies. Which is yet another reason why you should work out, since exercise is a natural way to help detox your system. Your blood circulates faster and more efficiently through the body when you exercise. As you work out, you take in more oxygen and you can rid your lungs of carbon dioxide as you breathe in more oxygenated air. Most times, you will feel better when you exercise and work up a sweat, I know I do!

So, even if time doesn't permit a workout, starting your day with meditation and deep breathing is *almost just* as good.

Body & Health

In order to be in balance and at peace within ourselves, we should also be aware of our physical bodies and overall health. Studies show that African-Americans develop high blood pressure at younger ages than other groups. High blood pressure leads to other serious illnesses such as heart disease, stroke and kidney disease.

As a young woman, I know you think you have time to get healthy when you get older. The fact of the matter is that the sooner you start out with healthy eating habits and a healthy lifestyle, the better your chances of carrying it into your future.

Be careful of the weight loss fads and exercise gimmicks. Look for the long term lifestyle benefits. Eat less fat, less salt, more fruits and vegetables and whole grains. Be active by going for walks, runs and register for Walk-a-thons. Your mind, body and spirit are all in one package. Take care of them all.

Silence and Stillness

With the hustle and bustle of the day, it is important that you take time to be still. There are many days that I drive in my car in complete silence. No radio, no talking on the Bluetooth, nothing but the sound of tires hitting the grooves in the road. When the mind is quiet, when there are no words to be said, we can literally hear our own heart talking to us. Peacefulness and still-ness generate the space for deep listening. It allows you to hear exactly what is spoken to you—the voice of insight and clarity that is normally silenced by internal noise and external busyness. Uncertainty diminishes, and your path becomes clearer.

With so much going on around us, we need to find a balance to be in harmony with our spirituality. Harmony includes a sense of association and attachment to all living beings and is linked to spirituality and religion. Harmony is happiness, complete-ness, fulfillment, satisfaction, acceptance, peace and aware-ness. There are different steps we have to take in order to be in harmony with ourselves. Most of these things we are familiar with, and yet, somehow we tend to avoid them. Maybe we are afraid to become the best versions of ourselves and to reach for our individual goals.

Fear

> *"I am deliberate and afraid of nothing. "*
>
> — *Audre Lorde*

Fear is your own worst enemy and with it, you will always stay at the same level, frustrated by your predicament. Every human being has fears. It's natural. Don't beat yourself up about your fears that you know are holding you back from achieving your goals.

Even animals have fears. However, the difference between hu-mans and animals is that animals fear an *immediate* danger and they position themselves to handle it or attack. Humans, on the other hand, spend most of our time worrying about what *could* happen.

Most people's fears have been rooted in them for so long that they don't recognize them as fears. Instead, they make statements like, "this is just who I am!" It's common to have a fear of failure, rejection or trust. What I've found to be the key to overcoming some of these critical fears is to first acknowledge them as a real fear. Second, by writing your fears down in your Royal Goals notebook, it makes you accountable to follow up on them and take action.

If your fear is of failure, then the best thing to do is to take small steps toward that main thing you are afraid of doing. For example, if its going back to school, why not take one online course? There are several on the web for a nominal fee or even free. Check the Resources Page at the end of this book to help in your search.

Think about that one thing you've always wanted to do. Is it to own a business? Write a book? Speak at a certain place? Work in a particular field? If so, then reach out to people who are doing any of the things that you currently fear. Their insight will be very helpful in your decision-making to go forward or change direction. After all, what's the worst that could happen? At least you will have found out what works for you early on and what doesn't. It is important to take certain risks as a young adult. You'd be surprised to know that some of the world's most successful people have failed — sometimes more than once. From

Walt Disney, to Oprah Winfrey and JK Rowling. Every great person has failed at something important to them at one point in their lives. Failure can be a great springboard to future success because of all of the lessons you learned.

> *"A crazy thing happened — the very act of doing the thing that scared me undid the fear. It's amazing the power of one word. 'Yes' changed my life. 'Yes' changed me."*
>
> — *Shonda Rhimes*

What about the millions of us who have a fear of rejection or never being good enough? I believe the same action steps apply. Write out your fears and become accountable to them. If you fear being told "No" for a job or an idea, find others who were also told "No" in similar circumstances. Research why a person or organization would say "No" to your situation. Think about what you can do differently to present your idea. One person's "No" may be another person's "Yes," so don't give up!

Finally, we all have moments where we do not feel qualified or good enough to go to the next level. Yet the ball is still in your court to increase your skill sets to speak for you and open doors. Be realistic about where you are in your career. Write out your plan to get to the next level and commit to it. Every new level requires more knowledge and life experiences. Knock out your fears of failure, rejection and not being good enough by taking small action steps to give you the confidence and momentum to shine.

Anxiety and Depression

According to the Anxiety and Depression Association, "anxiety disorders are the most common mental illness in the U.S. affecting 40 million adults age 18 and older.[1]" The good news is that most anxiety disorders are treatable, yet most people never get treated, for fear of labels or embarrassment.

These two common mental illnesses affects people of all ages, gender, races or social status. Depression affects your mood, how you feel each day and how you handle your daily activities. If you are in a "slump," more than you feel content with life, then you may be depressed. Signs may include:

- Dragging yourself out of bed each morning;
- Loss of appetite;
- Loss of energy;
- Long periods of sadness or loneliness;
- Trouble concentrating; or
- Isolating yourself from friends and other social activities.

Experts say if you are in this type of "slump" for at least *two weeks*, you should reach out to a professional organization for help with anxiety and depression. A few are noted in the Resources Pages at the end of this book.

I think it's great that many celebrities are opening about their personal struggles with anxiety and depression. It is a clear sign that no one's public success or wealth immunes them from mental illness. It takes a village to help one another and we are all in this together.

We must accept the fact that we are all spiritual beings. We all have an inner voice that helps us make decisions each day and choose right or wrong paths. By making time to meditate and being still for a few moments each day, you can bring clarity to stressful situations. Relax and take control of your mind, body and spirit one day at a time.

Mirror, Mirror

Queen Stephanie Brown James

Co-Founder, Vestige Strategies & Brown Girls Lead
Former NAACP College Director & Former Leader of
President Barack Obama's
Black Voter Outreach

The world has seen that there's not much Stephanie Brown James can't do! When she was 31 years old she was selected to Barack Obama's team as the lead director for Operation Vote, a national drive to increase voter registration among Black female, Latina, veteran and young people to the polls. Prior to that role, Stephanie was the National Director of the NAACP's Youth and College Division.

Later, Stephanie founded, Brown Girls Lead, a seven-month leadership initiative for girls at Howard University. The program was in place for five years and has supported the leadership development of over 200 women in the Washington, D.C. area.

Today, along with her husband Quentin, she is the Co-Founder of Vestige Strategies, a public affairs firm that specializes in grassroots engagements and political campaigns. Stephanie has dedicated her life to making a difference in the lives of the least counted while empowering women and communities of color. Stephanie is a woman who credits everything in her life to her faith in God, as she juggles a number of business responsibilities, including being a wife and mother. Also, she is a woman who sees a need in the marketplace or community and directs her time and energy toward making an immediate impact. What skill sets are you using to make a difference in your life? In the lives of others?

Queen's Wisdom

*"There's always something to suggest that
you'll never be who you wanted to be.
Your choice is to take it or keep on moving."*
— **Phylicia Rashad**

As you know by now, life can be challenging. Whether you are dealing with time management, money management or people management, it is bound to bring about stress and unexpected circumstances.

Having a spiritual foundation where you can meditate, have quiet time, read or listen to soothing music are great habits to begin now. Likewise, eating healthier and staying active are beneficial to your spiritual well-being.

★ Make time each day to be still and meditate for 10 or 15 minutes to have clarity throughout the day.

★ Trust your moral compass to make the right decisions when pressured to do something you know is wrong.

★ Don't let fear hold you back from at least trying to accomplish a goal. You will never know the *real* outcome if you don't try. Take small steps to achieve the larger goal.

★ Failure is inevitable in doing something new. Learn from it. Don't make the same mistakes. Continue to move forward.

★ Set realistic expectations for your goals. Know what it takes to get where you want to go, and work hard to get there. No excuses.

★ If you are withdrawing from others, have no energy, no appetite, or are experiencing sadness or loneliness, for a few weeks, chances are you are suffering from anxiety or depression. Talk to someone you trust or contact a professional who can direct you to get the help you need.

Working to strike a balance between your spirituality, and your mind and body all require a committed effort on your part to be at peace. Your overall well-being is critical to accepting your role as a queen. #Dailyspiritualitycheckup.

APP#4
SELF-EMPOWERMENT
FOUNDATION

#Wakandanwomenrock

*"Trust yourself. Think for yourself.
Act for yourself. Speak for yourself.
Be yourself. Imitation is suicide."*

– Marva Collins

As young adults, you all have to get to a point where you take full responsibility for your life's path. Your actions, inactions or growth are ultimately in your hands. Any detours, mistakes or do-overs, rest solely upon yourself. That's really what self-empowerment is all about - taking control of your life, setting and achieving goals, and making the right decisions. Doing these things should give you a sense of fulfilment and peace.

Many people spend their entire life pleasing others, going along with the crowd, and trying to fit in. These people-pleasers lack self-empowerment skills to move past other's goals and opinions of them. Your life belongs to you. You have the power to control key aspects of your life. Don't give away your power to those who do not care about you, are not part of your future and have done nothing to uplift or encourage you. Take back your power!

Of course, we don't have all the answers to our life's puzzle, but we must make a deliberate effort to put the pieces in place to help us create the big picture.

What are you doing now to help your future growth?

What steps are you taking towards finding your purpose?

What are your strongest skills sets?

What areas are you lacking?

Answer these questions honestly. It will only help you as you move forward. Believe me, I know it's hard at a young age to figure out what you want to do. However, it becomes easier when you start by looking at the things that you like, but more importantly, to those things that come natural for you. Keep in mind that this exercise is not intended for you to figure out what you want to do for the rest of your life. Instead, it's the roadmap for next year and the year after that. Once you have a two year plan, then future plans for change and growth will become easier. *What if you don't have the confidence to grow?* Like anything new, self-empowerment can be learned.

There are literally millions of books and articles on finding your purpose and self-empowerment. In actuality, there is a real difference between feeling empowered and being empowered. I must admit, I have read several books on self-empowerment. Yet I'm not sure if they helped me move farther along my own path.

Sure, after reading these types of books, I am initially gung-ho about making the changes to one or two areas in my life, but for some reason, life gets in the way and I revert back to my own version of self-empowerment. It's not that what I am doing is wrong or ineffective, it's that change is hard and can sometimes be painful. I stick to my plan better when it is on my terms, rather than someone else's. That's why it is so important to be open and honest with yourself about your goals and objectives towards change and ultimately self-leadership. Below are a few tips to consider if you believe you are lacking the confidence to work towards self-empowerment:

Tip #1

Acknowledgment & Self-Awareness - Most of the time we are in denial of our true character. In order to fully embrace your new self-empowerment walk, you must come clean about your strengths, weaknesses and what really makes you "tick." Again, spending time alone in meditation where you can relax and have a clearer picture of the real you will help in this process. The objective of this first tip is for you to be truthful.

Tip #2

Belief System/Moral Compass - How you were raised, your family traditions and values are key factors in your self-empowerment journey. Your moral compass became active as a child when you understood right from wrong. Stand up for what you believe in. Associate with those that have similar values, yet don't judge others who share different values from you. Don't allow others opinions of you, change your beliefs or views of yourself.

Tip #3

Change of Mindset - In order to really wear your new self-empowerment crown, you need to be open to a changed mindset. No more worrying about the past or the future. You have to trust yourself and your instincts about situations. Shifting your mindset to a more positive focus on outcomes is also key. This goes back to our earlier discussion on how changing your outlook on a situation can change the world. Learn from others. Share your ideas. Be bold. Be open. Be confident.

Tip #4

Action Goals - At this stage, the goals that you write down should be action-oriented, with tasks and completion dates. Such goals can include increasing your knowledge or skill sets in certain areas, networking, volunteering, writing affirmations or any new and active role you need to engage in towards growth and becoming more empowered.

Mirror, Mirror

Three Queens
The Black Panther Movie

Although **The Black Panther** is a fictional movie, its national and international box office success demonstrates that African-American actors have star power and the world has been waiting for us to put our talents on display.

The entire movie provides viewers with a sense of empowerment and pride of their African heritage, and defies Hollywood stereotypes. Yet the total bonus of the movie is the depiction of strong black female characters: Shuri, Okoye and Nakia.

Shuri, although a teenager, is a tech genius with her own laboratory to invent gadgets to improve the lives of Wakandans and the world at large. She is intelligent, beautiful, funny and does not let the word "No" stop her from finding the right solution.

Okoye is not only a physically strong and gifted warrior, she is intelligent and loyal. She trusts her own instincts and is willing to fight for what she believes in.

Finally, Nakia is the one that most young women can relate to. She fell in love with a Prince, yet she did not let her love for him deter her dreams of helping those less fortunate. She is a great example of what it means to stay true to your goals and values.

All three of these strong Black female characters demonstrate self-empowerment on every level: they are confident, they took control of their lives, they are committed to their values, they made positive decisions and they took active steps to achieve their next level goals. You can do the same. You have the same qualities of all three of these women. You rock! #Wakandanwomenrock!

Queen's Wisdom

We all have "what if" fears. Yet once we move past the doubts, we can focus on improving our current situation. It won't happen overnight, but if you practice the steps to increasing your self-confidence, you can embark upon your self-empowerment journey with ease.

★ Be proactive in your self-empowerment journey. Take small reasonable steps each day, each week, to gain confidence towards achieving your goal.

★ Be honest and realistic in what you desire to accomplish based on where you are today.

★ You must put a stake in the ground and take control of your life. There is no time like the present! #Trustyourinstinctsuseyourpower.

APP #5

BEAUTY FOUNDATION

#Youareabeautifulqueen

"I am not my hair
I am not this skin
I am a soul that
lives within."

— *India Arie*

"**B**eautiful!" The one word that all women want to be called at some point in their lives. It's a word that has defined a women's view of her future for centuries. Society inflicts its male perception of beauty upon us and we pressure ourselves to achieve those outward expectations of beauty. It is unavoidable for the majority of women not to think about beauty; our facial features, our hair, our body image or our style of dress. All of these physical characteristics can be stressful and expensive to maintain. Especially since we are bombarded by images in the media, magazines, commercials and billboards, dictating every aspect of how we should look.

It's not just the media that is involved in the business of beauty; everyone around us is constantly talking about the latest trends and celebrity style and there are thousands of beauty and fashion blogs. Social media has fueled the tension even more with sites like Facebook and Instagram, challenging women to post their best selfies.

As teens, you are targeted by the media because they believe you are vulnerable and will buy into their messages. The media's beauty standard is unrealistic and superficial. It deprives you of a true understanding of how to care for and dress your body. Black women are targeted negatively with messages that we are just not beautiful enough.

For decades, we have been told that our skin color, hair texture and body features don't fit the norm. Black girls are being sent home from school for wearing natural hairstyles under the pretense of being against the school code. Black women are being penalized at work for wearing natural styles under the guise of violating the corporate dress code. Everything that is unique about us is being dictated by what one group has considered the societal norm, which is actually more European. We must remain true to who we are on both the outside and inside.

Young girls growing up today don't realize how difficult it was to find a successful female role model in the fashion industry when I was growing up during the 70 and 80s. A woman of color's worth was defined by the shade of her skin. We watched as the media labeled us the inferior beauty symbol. But not anymore! You are just one of the black queens all over the world who no longer buy into mainstream media's narrative of beauty. It's up to you to create your *own* standard.

Uniquely Made

Unfortunately, most of our view is beauty is defined by today's slender models, actresses and celebrities with European features. Many girls receive THE FALSE MESSAGE THAT THIN EQUALS BEAUTY. In fact many females never feel slim enough! When I was younger I also believed this for many years until my junior high school teacher, who later became my sorority sister, told me, "you were created to be unique, you are not supposed to be like the women on TV. People will like you because of who you are and not just because of your outer appearance." I never forgot those magical, life-changing words. I wish more African-American girls heard these powerful words so they would be as comfortable as I became in my own skin.

Body Image

Like many females, I would love to have been born with a different body type. Definitely taller, with longer leaner legs and overall thin in appearance. But I wasn't. I have learned to buy clothes that make me look like I am all those things. It's taken me many years and trial and error to come to that clothing style trick.

Each of us has our own body flaws, too skinny, too fat, too tall or too thin. It's difficult to find a female on planet Earth who's totally happy with her body. Instead of torturing yourself over what it is you do not like, be realistic about what you can and cannot change. Of course it is possible to gain or lose weight. And yes, like millions of other females, I would love to be ten or fifteen pounds lighter. Although it's not possible to make yourself taller or shorter, how you dress and carry yourself can send out a totally different perception of your body size. I will never stop monitoring my weight or exercising, but I refuse to let myself get totally miserable about it either. Trust me, life is too short.

> *"You can be whatever size you are, and you can be beautiful both inside and out."*
>
> **— Serena Williams**

Black beauty is so unique and magnificent. There is no denying our bold statement with our presence. Our defined lips, kinky-curly hair, broad nose and everything else on the inside is what makes us who we are. Royalty! Don't let anyone tell you that who you are is not enough. For me, my mother's words kept me through my days of condemnation. When people told me,

I would be better if I was taller and thinner: I reminded myself that it's just their opinion. Never allow people's limited views shape your identity. You are definitely more than what the world says about you.

Another part of me that I struggled to accept is my hair. My mom kept my hair natural during my younger years. I wore the typical little girl braids or two plaits with barrettes and colorful ribbons at the ends. However, during my upper teen years, I discovered relaxers and extensions. I made hair choices because I wanted to, not to look like anyone else. I liked a relaxed look and I went for it. Does it define me? No, it does not. How you wear your hair is your choice. What you wear is your choice. Fashion trends are always changing but your personal style remains yours. Gone are the days when we were pressured to perm our hair and wear extension just to be accepted. Now, you can choose how you want to look. Whether you decide to relax your hair, wear it natural or get extensions: it's all about what you feel comfortable in. There are great black beauty blogger, vloggers, and social media influencers; inspiration is all around you to provide advice.

Don't pay attention to the white-dominated media's version of your identity. Social media has given you a platform to get connected with other women of color. You need to know that beauty is skin deep. Self-confidence is what defines beauty. Makeup is not meant to cover your beauty, its intended to enhance it.

"She is Black Girl Excellence. She is Me."

— *Stephanie Lahart*

Be indifferent to the people who constantly try to put you down. No one can make you feel less than without your permission. When you take people's opinions too seriously, you give them power over your life. You were made to stand out and your personality is not over the top or too much. You, my black queen are neither your body shape, hair texture or your skin tone. You are a beautiful soul.

Styled by You

As a teen, you may not have a clear view of your personal style yet, but that's alright. Experiment with your clothes. Try different things - when you find what works for you, stick to it.

Become bold enough to know that your actions, personality and identity speak louder than your hair, clothes or makeup. If you are struggling with confidence be sure to hook up with other women of color on the internet who have experienced similar challenges. You'll be surprised how supportive people can be. Looking good is great, but if you let your clothes define you, you'll struggle to accept your true personality later in life.

> *"Confidence, is always the best accessory.*
> *Own the moment. Own your space."*
>
> **— Andrena Sawyer**

Wear your personality, not just your clothes. You do not need to buy expensive clothes to feel worthy of attention. If you can't afford it now, shop at affordable stores that carry good, stylish clothes. There are many inexpensive brands like H&M that sell quality clothes. Browse YouTube when you need style inspiration.

It is OK to have celebrity style inspiration, but make sure to choose clothes that suit you, and makes you feel beautiful, instead of just what's trending. Unless you want to get a career in the fashion industry, I advise girls to stop focusing too much on fashion. You can be inspired by other people's style - but avoid becoming a copy. The key to dressing right is knowing your body type: know what fits you and what does not. Remember that fashion does not define us, we create fashion. Be confident on the inside, no matter how good the clothes look on the outside.

Black Beauty Means Business

Today, we are the leaders of the $7.5 billion Black beauty industry. No longer do you have to deal with rejection based upon your outward appearance, because strong Black women have gone before you to make it easier for you to find inner self-love and outer self-beauty geared to your natural tones. Nearly every major beauty brand has created or is in the process of introducing darker skin tones for makeup and hundreds of health and beauty products relevant to our needs.

Black women celebrities are the faces of major brands like CoverGirl featuring Queen Latifah, Tyra Banks, Janelle Monáe, the cast of Empire and several others. Not to mention in 2017, Rihanna launched Fenty Beauty which is on pace to be the highest selling brand amongst African-Americans and Hispanics. There is power in your spending. Use your power wisely.

I love how makeup can totally transform a person's look in a way that nothing else can. Experimenting with makeup, watching YouTube, and keeping up on new makeup trends is a great way to update your look. That being said, I don't believe women *have* to wear makeup to look beautiful. In fact, in the past few years, some celebrities have made a huge statement with their, "no makeup" campaigns. Some women I know prefer to go natural and I think that's awesome. I've even gotten away from wearing makeup every day. If you're comfortable being makeup-free, more power to you!

Skin Tone Conversation

"Beauty shouldn't be defined by whether you wear the Deepest Deep Foundation (like me!) or the Translucent one. It's all about confidence in your own skin and in your beauty. It's corny, but it's true."

— Jayne Mandat

Unfortunately, skin tone is still a hotly debated issue amongst the Black community. Dark-skinned versus light-skinned continue to surface because historically, skin tone had a social and economic status attached to it, and it holds true today. Lighter skinned individuals have been labeled or perceived by the mainstream as more attractive than those with darker skin. Past studies showed that lighter skinned employees received promotions or other company benefits over a darker skinned employee.

Celebrities in various arenas are bleaching their skin with creams and intravenous medical treatments, causing outrage and concern within the Black community. However, we should not judge a woman's decision to change her physical appearance because we have no idea what has happened in her life to cause her to make that decision. Whether she chooses skin bleaching, hair extensions, implants, gastric bypass or any other cosmetic surgery, it's personal and her choice. As long as she has an abundance of self-love and love for others, that is what really matters.

R-E-S-P-E-C-T

"Deal with yourself as an individual worthy of respect

and make everyone else deal with you the same way."

— Nikki Giovanni

Carry yourself with respect and do not accept anything less from others. My advice is that you use your teen years to focus on building your self-confidence. Write out daily affirmations in your Royal Goals book. Every time that negative voice comes along, shut it down immediately, and speak something positive into your day. Always dress to make your most beautiful features more prominent. Big corporations have succeeded in deceiving us that we need to wear their products to feel beautiful, but we don't. Learn how to use makeup if it makes you happy.

Healthy Lifestyle

Beauty comes from belief first. Second, your physical and mental health. We talked briefly about the importance of a healthy mind and body in an earlier chapter. Yes, girl, you should eat healthy and workout. You are going to waste a lot of money buying products to work miracles if you do not start eating healthy now. You need the right amount of fruits and vegetables, that have antioxidants to make your skin glow.

You Are What You Eat

Eating junk food not only makes you sick, it gives you skin problems, makes you feel tired and does little to improve your overall health. You are never too young to pay attention to what you feed your body. I've seen students in my school first thing in the morning drinking orange soda and eating Swedish Fish. What a shock to your system! There are so many studies which show that breakfast is the most important meal that you can eat before school. Unfortunately, most kids skip a nutritious breakfast and settle for junk food or nothing. What young people don't realize is that eating properly helps you to develop mentally and physically. When your body does not get the proper nutrients, you won't feel good and your moods will be off balance.

To be at your best health, every day make sure you get the right amount protein (eggs, fish, chicken, vegetables), carbohydrates (fruits, vegetables, potatoes, pasta, rice), and fruit. Protein helps your muscles, hair, skin, eyes and internal organs. Basically, you need protein to grow. Our bodies also need the right amount of fat to be healthy. There are both good and bad fats. Good fats include nuts, fresh tuna and salmon. Bad fats are found in those produced from animals like dairy products and meats which should be eaten in moderation.

Try eating healthy/balanced meals and see if it makes a difference in your energy level as well as sharpen your mind. Cut out the sugary drinks and soda from your diet as continued use can increase your risk of type 2 diabetes, high blood pressure, obesity or other health ailments that disproportionately affect African-Americans.

Being healthy will change your life. I never used to believe it until I started working out. I felt more confident about my body and maintained my weight. You too can achieve good health and happiness by joining a sports team at school or starting a workout routine. Playing competitive sports is good for your confidence, keeps you in shape and improves your mood. Scientists have found that being active (working out) makes the brain release feel-good hormones known as endorphins: these hormones improve your mood, keep your mind active, helps you stop worrying and protects your brain. Beauty is not just about the clothes, makeup, and products; it's about your overall health. You should strive to live a healthy life - the sooner the better.

Another important piece of advice is to use natural skin care products. Most store-bought brands are full of chemicals which builds up and could lead to serious health problems in the long run. Aloe Vera, shea butter and natural black soap are good alternatives for girls and women of color. When buying products choose those based on what suits your skin type. If you have dry skin, you should be more concerned about keeping your skin moisturized. If it's oily, you want to stay away from heavy products. For normal skin, follow the directions on the more standard products. The melanin in your skin does not affect your skin type. Skin tone only matters when you are choosing your makeup, not products.

Also, it's possible to have more than one skin type, especially on the face. Glowing skin should be the goal of your skincare regime. It's okay to try products to see what works for you, but don't become a product junky. Trust me these companies are not always truthful when they state that their latest creams will *"magically"* change your life. Decide what works for you and incorporate it into your daily skin care routine.

Many girls and women of color often forget when it comes to skin care that they need to wear sunblock or use products with sun protection factor (SPF). Yes, our darker skin tone is meant to protect us from the harmful rays of the sun, but because of the depleting ozone layer, we are just as susceptible to sunburn as fair-skinned people. According to the data from Centre for Disease Control (CDC), Black men and women are less likely to die from skin cancer or sun exposure. Regardless, be proactive and use SPF. It will shield you from the sun's harmful rays by forming a protective layer around the surface of your skin.

At the end of the day, beauty is in the eye of the beholder. If you believe that you are beautiful on the inside and out, then you are! #Youareabeautifulqueen.

Mirror, Mirror

Queen Kheris Rogers
#FlexinInMyComplexion

When 11-year-old entrepreneur Kheris Rogers was younger, she often asked her older sister if she could stay in the bathtub longer in hopes of lightening her skin tone. Throughout elementary school, Kheris was darker than the other black girls in school. She was bullied and teased because of her dark complexion daily.

When she was 10, Kheris' older sister posted a photo of Kheris on Twitter in a black dress with red and green print and a beautiful curly natural hair style. The photo was captioned "My sister is only 10, but already royalty. #FlexinInHerComplexion. That post received over 100,000 retweets and likes.

At that moment, with the social media support, media attention, Kheris and her older sister Taylor Pollard, became co-CEO's of the FlexinInMyComplexion company. They have sold thousands of T-shirts, jackets, and accessories.

Kheris turned a negative and stressful bullying situation into a positive inspiration for other young girls to follow. Young, beautiful, intelligent, Kheris Rogers, is a true example of self-empowerment, black beauty and business sense. Check out Kheris' products at https://www.flexininmycomplexion.com/.

Queen's Wisdom

It's hard escape the beauty conversation in our daily lives. Since birth, our value has been defined by another person's perception of our beauty, even within our own family. We are all pre-programmed to put labels on others based on their appearance. Whether you have been labeled beautiful or have been labeled something negative, neither should matter because outward appearances are usually false or misleading. What you're made of on the inside will determine long-term happiness and success according to your standards.

★ You are an unique one-of-a-kind original. Don't waste time trying to be someone else.

★ Spend your dollars wisely. You have power to control the narrative of what Black girl beauty looks like.

★ Wear clothing that compliments your body and create your own style.

★ Whatever your hair texture, embrace it, yet try new things to make you happy. Whether it's wearing it natural, a perm or extensions, be comfortable and confident in your choice.

★ Treat everyone with respect, regardless of their skin tone. Don't become a person who treats her sister differently because she is light-skinned or dark-skinned.

★ It's important to also take care of our bodies and begin to care about what you eat for each meal. Add more fruits and vegetables daily and cut back on sugary drinks and junk food.

APP# 6
GIRLFRIEND FOUNDATION
#Sisterhoodislifechanging

*"No person is your friend who demands
your silence, or denies your right to grow."*

— Alice Walker

Nothing can replace the true sacred sisterhood of a girlfriend. We were all created to be in special relationships with one another through communication and our actions. As females, we bond and connect with our sisters to create acquaintances or lasting friendships. Many of us have girlfriends since elementary school years. We give true meaning to BFF.

Girlfriends are there for you through the good times and bad. They have a front row seat to all of your relationship cycles: single, dating, husband, divorce and often times single again. They are the ones who can tell you the truth and make you laugh, cry and sing all within a matter of minutes. They can get you off the couch and motivate you to be your best. Every moment with your girlfriends becomes a memorable shared experience that you treasure for a lifetime.

All relationships can be complicated! At the same time, for most girls, female relationships are especially important. There are days that you will really need support and advice that can only come from a girlfriend. We all need friends we can depend on. All of my closet friendships have had a dynamic impact on who I am today. We accomplish more together because my friends can be strong for me when I'm weak, and I can be strong for them when they are weak. Different friends can help you in different ways, too. I have one friend whom I can laugh with for hours. I have another friend who is super wise and always gives great advice. Each friend brings something special to my life in a different way.

Who is in your girlfriend circle and why?

How do you invest in your girlfriends?

I've found that the best way to maintain genuine friendships is to be friendly, nurture others and be a good listener. Everyone needs a shoulder to cry on, lean on or just be in the room for support at some point in their life.

BFF Benefits

There are so many positive effects of having girlfriends. First, studies show that women with close relationships to girlfriends live longer than those who don't have strong connections with other women. Second, women who have girlfriend bonds have less stress as they are able to vent and air out their issues with their friends who they believe really get their issue. They have time to spend together and do fun and relaxing things like going shopping, to a spa or weekend retreats. Third, self-esteem increases in women as based upon a study by Dove, which showed that 70% of women stated they felt prettier by having close girlfriends.

> *"Lots of people want to ride with you in the limo,*
> *but you want someone who will take the bus with*
> *you when the limo breaks down."*
> *- Oprah Winfrey*

Again, having girlfriends is such an important and healthy part of your relationship circle. A psychiatrist at Stanford University gave a lecture in which he said one of the best things a woman can do for her health is to nurture her relationships with her girlfriends. Women connect with each other to deal with life's stress and other situations. We lean on each other. We depend on each other to listen, provide advice, comfort and to just be there when we need them.

There is even medical evidence to demonstrate this bonding benefit. Girlfriend time is really quality time where serotonin is created in our neurotransmitters to make use feel good and fight depression. Female friendships include sharing in each other's lives. Most times, no subject is off limits with your girlfriend. She is the one that gets you when no one else does.

There are ways that can help you strengthen your friendship with your girlfriends. By practicing the five suggestions listed below, you can build meaningful, long lasting relationships.

1. Be your authentic self. The topic is common sense, yet living it out is difficult to do. Let's face it, we live in a world that expects girls to be perfect. Who wants to admit they're falling short of the ideal? But the reality is nobody's life is a constant dream. No human will ever be close to perfect. The real you attracts real friends, so be honest about yourself in person and online.

2. Don't sweat the small things.

3 Control your jealousy.

4. Keep the lines of communication open.

5. Show appreciation.

Sororities and Sisterhood

Sororities and Sisterhood — There are many benefits to sorority membership, but few are greater than the unconditional and lifetime bonds of friendship that we call sisterhood.

Greta Hendricks Johnson explains the history of African-American Sororities:

"Sororities are generally defined as a college social groups or organization for women, with particular distinction given to African -American sororities. Birthed at a time in history when the traditional roles of women were being challenged, the founders of the first Black sororities had to overcome the stereotypical views of sexism and racism as well. These young women were considered exceptional in their own considering that a college education was not easily accessible to African Americans. By contrast, within mainstream society they were subject to rejection because of the color of their skin, having to prove their capabilities in the intellectual environment of the collegiate world. The need arose to organize a support system, the horizontal ties known as sisterhood. Destined to become leaders, nine women stood strong and formed the first African American sorority in 1908."

Today, hundreds of years later—and thousands strong—we vow to continue the legacy of our founders by standing together with a lifetime commitment in support of education, integrity, activism and public service.

You probably won't be surprised to know that K. Michelle was a member of a Sorority, but what about Mrs. Coretta Scott King? Take a look at some of the most prominent African-American sorority members. An expanded list is included in the Clubs& Organizations section of this book.

***

Alicia Keys- Alicia became an honorary member of the historic Alpha Kappa Alpha Sorority in 2004.

Keisha Knight Pulliam- This former "Cosby" kid joined the Delta Sigma Theta sorority while attending Spelman College.

Towanda Braxton- Actress and producer, Towanda is a proud member of Zeta Phi Beta sorority, Inc.

Lana "Mc Lyte" Moore- Female rap legend and co-founder of the Hip Hop Sisters Foundation, Lana "MC Lyte" is a proud member of Sigma Gamma Rho Sorority, Inc.

AKA

Alpha Kappa Alpha Sorority, Inc. (AKA), the oldest Greek-letter organization established for African American women, was founded on January 15, 1908, on the campus of Howard University in Washington, D.C. The principles are Sisterhood, Scholarship and Service to All Humankind. This organization was founded on two key themes. The first is the importance of the individual. The second is the strength of an organization of women of ability and courage. The sorority formed to serve an African-American community that faced the growing challenge of racial discrimination and injustice in the early 20th Century United States.

It's tough to explain what a women's sorority truly means to us. In fact, sisterhood is so many things all wrapped up into a beautiful package – one of the most heartfelt & life-changing things in the world!

Sisterhood is being there to encourage one another through good times and when we're having a bad day or going through tough times.

Sisterhood is a pat on the back, a friendly hug or a cheerful hello.

Sisterhood is about doing the little things to make our sisters smile.

Sisterhood is knowing that there will always be someone around whom you can talk to or share your stories with, no matter what.

Sisterhood is about sharing dreams and achieving goals together. In addition, it's aspiring to reach greater heights and exceed expectations together.

Sisterhood is about counting on others and being counted on to make a difference.

Sisterhood is more than the letters which we wear around campus – it's something much greater, something sacred and treasured.

Sisterhood is showing and telling others the good that we do; likewise, it's showing and telling others the lasting impacts that we're making for the better for our colleges/universities and communities.

Sisterhood is learning about people. It's about learning about life. It's about learning to give back to our campuses and communities selflessly.

Simply put, it's the ultimate experience of a lifetime – an experience unlike any other! As a proud member of Alpha Kappa Alpha Sorority, Inc., I can honestly say that sisterhood is truly all of these things listed above and so much more! #Sisterhoodislifechanging.

Mirror, Mirror

The Cast of *Girls Trip, 2017*

Girls Trip will go down in history as the comedy that will forever remind us of the importance of our girlfriends and reigniting those friendships. Based on real life events of friends going to the *Essence Music Festival* in New Orleans, *Girls Trip* leaves nothing on the table: true friendship, laughs, respect and love for each other.

The spot on casting left audiences relating to each female character in the movie. Everyone has a girlfriend circle with a Ryan (up and coming celebrity), Lisa (uptight nurse and mom), Sasha (former career success) and Dina (crazy friend, never takes life seriously).

Girls Trip reminds us that we all need to reconnect with our girlfriends no matter how many years have passed. It is a funny, yet realistic film that clearly displays that nothing in our careers, romantic relationships, or life's challenges, can take the place of true sisterhood.

Queen's Wisdom

★ Surround yourself with girlfriends who love you and want to see you grow.

★ Your girlfriend circle should always be a safe zone to be yourself and share without judgment.

★ The more honest and authentic you are with your girlfriends, the more fulfilling your relationship will be.

★ Sisters help each other in good times and bad. Make yourself available to be a shoulder to lean or cry on.

★ Sororities are a great way to bond with sisters with similar goals and values.

★ Sisterhood has many positive effects for your physical and mental well-being.

APP #7
MONEY FOUNDATION

#Smartfemaleshandlefinances

"You can only become truly accomplished at something you love. Don't make money your goal. Instead, pursue the things you love doing, and then do them so well that people can't take their eyes off you."

— *Maya Angelou*

By now you should be concerned about money. Understanding the value of money and how to manage it is a learned process. We just don't automatically know what to do with it. Our instinct is to spend it as soon as it touches our hands or shows up in our bank account. Most teenagers are caught up in the "want" phase and *want* every new gadget, clothing, shoes or other thing that comes along. Working within a budget is not something that feels good, yet it is probably one of the most important skills you can acquire and master.

Financial knowledge is not something taught in the majority of schools today, so it is up to you to learn about it on your own. I say this because, realistically your parents may not have been taught. Nearly all financial experts advise you to pay yourself first. Whether you get an allowance, gift money or a paycheck, always put aside something for yourself for the future. In order to begin earning money you need a job. To get a job it is important to have a resume. It shows potential employers that you are serious about your future.

Your Resume

If you are like most girls your age, you probably have not given much thought to preparing a resume. Resumes are not just for parents, teachers and people with careers. As a young adult, you will find that a resume is your ticket to finding a job and eventually a career. You will use your resume when applying for internships, training programs or college.

A resume is a short summary of a person's accomplishments and qualifications. Your first resume helps you:

i)   Keep track of your education and work experiences;

ii) Recognize and highlight your skills and interests; and

iii) Save time by attaching your resume to online applications instead filling out the paper forms for every company.

If you don't have a resume, you won't have a neat organized way to let people know about your education, experience and skills. A good resume makes it easy for you to share this information whenever you need to.

In addition, your interests outside of school, such as baby-sitting, working on computers, or doing hair and makeup may lead you to pursue paid or volunteer work. This type of work experience will strengthen your resume and help you decide if this job is something you would like to do for a career.

Many employers will be impressed if you have a resume as a high school student or recent grad. You can use several different methods to submit a resume. Many employers now ask that you send your resume by email. You can also apply for jobs online by copying and pasting your resume into an online resume builder that the company supplies. You should have a resume both on paper and in an electric format and ready to present as needed.

Most people change their careers and jobs many times during their lives, especially when they are just getting started. If you change your mind about your interest in a certain type of work, make sure you update your resume.

The Interview: Are You Ready?

So they liked your resume. Today is the big day. You have an appointment for an interview. Be calm and relaxed. Here are a few pointers to keep in mind:

- Be on time, actually, plan to arrive a few minutes early.
- Bring a pen and notebook.
- Be prepared and research the company before the interview.
- Wear nice clothes (no jeans) that fit the company's image.
- Wear very little or no perfume. Some people may be allergic to perfumes.
- Sell yourself. Don't be afraid to make yourself sound great.
- Look your interviewer in the eye, don't look down.
- Smile when you can.
- Watch your posture and don't put your hands in your pockets.
- Ask questions.
- Be polite and thank the interviewer for his or her time.

Money Habits

As you get older, your expenses will be greater. When you add up teen expenses besides life's necessities like food, clothing and shelter, and include organized sports and school events, you will see that money and expenses add up quickly. This is also a time when you start dating and going out with your friends on weekends. Hanging out with your friends and pitching in for gas or your own car expenses can be tough. There are a few money lessons where experts agree:

i) Earning Income: If you work after school and on weekends, decide how you are going to save and spend your paycheck *before* you get it. Open both a savings and checking account. You should also get a debit card to help curb your spending habits; you can't spend what you don't have. However, don't link your debit card to your savings or you will find yourself broke by transferring funds on your phone between both accounts. Many banks require a guardian to sign off on withdrawals if you are under age 18.

ii) Creating a Budget: Write out your spending needs for the week or every two weeks depending on your pay period. Subtract your expenses from your income. With state and federal taxes, you will see that you don't have as much as you thought. Chances are you will have a shortfall. What things can you do or cut out to break even, or put aside for savings?

iii) Saving for the future: Make a list of things you desire for the future. Pay yourself and stick to your budget to purchase the item. Don't deplete your savings all at once. Be patient.

iv) Shopping: Shopping can be rewarding or satisfying. We buy stuff we need. We buy stuff we want. As females, we just like shopping. A few key things to remember is i) Buy out of season;

ii) Shop from the clearance rack; and iii) Use coupons and discount cards.

Saving for Retirement, IRAs, 401Ks, etc.

With the high cost of living today, it is difficult for most people to save, let alone think about saving for their future. Even though you are young, familiarizing yourself with retirement concepts will expose you to a few common saving options. Many employers offer 401(k) retirement savings plans which require you to contribute a specific amount from your paycheck each pay period. This is a good "forced" way to save without taxes being taken out, until you withdraw the money.

Some employers match your contributions as well. If you choose to work in an educational field, a non-profit organization, or hospital cooperative, your employer will likely offer a 403(b) retirement savings plan with similar functions as a 401(k). Keep in mind that the terms 401(k) and 403(b) all refer to that particular section of the Internal Revenue Code. Each of these sections provides a lot of detail on the maximum contributions and other rules for opening an account to receive tax benefits under that code.

There are other employer plans, as well as special plans for business owners, so make sure you inquire about additional options to see which plan will work best for you. As an individual, other retirement saving options such as an IRA or a Roth IRA can be purchased from your bank or other financial institution. Saving for retirement and investing can be both confusing and rewarding. Make sure you review the plan information and then talk with your employer's human resources department or a local financial professional, before you open any type of retirement savings account, as there are risks involved.

Make learning how to manage your money a priority. Read books on money management and use the available tools and apps to help get you started on the right track.

Independent Living

As a teenager, I could not wait to get out of my parents' house. I thought having my own place would be the best thing in the world. I was wrong. Living on your own is a huge responsibility. First, you have to be great at budgeting and sticking to it. The due date for bills come around quickly; rent, car insurance, electricity, cable, cell phone, groceries, gas, or other necessities. What about those who have student loans and credit card debt? Do you realize that on any given month, six or more bills could be due around the same time? How can you afford to pay them?

I recall being short on funds every month. I asked my dad for money often. I did not have a plan so I just winged things until it was obvious that I needed to move back home. Once I saved up and was ready the second time around, I made a list of my expenses and included cushion for emergencies. The list also included expenses for clothing, eating out and going to the movies. Make it realistic so you can see where you need to cut back, save, and not put yourself in the hole each month. Living on your own may mean hanging out and eating out less. You will have to sacrifice.

You cannot live on your own unless you have a job. Depending on the area, you may need two jobs to live comfortably. A landlord will not rent their place to you if you do not have a steady income. Since you are starting out, many will require an established person to co-sign the apartment in case you fail to pay the rent. In most cases, it is a good idea to have a roommate to split all of the living costs equally. Count up the costs before you venture out on your own. Talk to others who have done it and listen to their advice and learn from their mistakes. If you are not mature and responsible in handling money, you will not live on your own for long. #Smartfemaleshandlefinances.

Time Management Success

Do you plan your week? People who do have a real advantage when it comes to organizing their time. Why? Well, more than any other time period, a block of seven days makes a time management schedule worth keeping. Once you know what your commitments consist of each week, you're able to manage your time far more effectively and efficiently. With that in mind, consider using a planner to help you organize your time. An example planner is provided for you in the back of this book.

Mirror, Mirror

Queen Stacey Tisdale

Founder, Mind Money Media

Young women today are fortunate to have an African-American female financial journalist with over 20 years' experience in Stacey Tisdale. As the President of Mind Money Media, she provides a financial educational curriculum to elementary through college-aged students in partnership with NFL Hall of Famer Ronnie Lott's, All Stars Helping Kids Foundation. She contributed to Lott's *Winning Play $* content, which consecutively won the U.S. Department of Education's Excellence in Economic Education Award. Stacey is also the author of *The True Cost of Happiness: The Real Story Behind Managing Your Money*.

Stacey has filed business and consumer reports for all of the CNN networks, including, CNN, CNNI and Headline News. Stacey has also contributed reports to "Money Talks," the nationally syndicated program created by BusinessWeek, and appeared on the "The Oprah Winfrey Show" as a financial expert and in *O Magazine.* She has also written for *Essence Magazine* and was Senior Editor of personal finance for *Black Enterprise.* To learn more about managing your finances or Stacey's programs, go to https://www.mindmoneymedia.com/.

Queens Wisdom

★ You are never too young to learn about managing money. The sooner you understand spending and saving, the better off you will be when you live on your own.

★ Always pay yourself first and put something aside for a rainy day.

★ Don't accept credit card offers until you have steady job or career.

★ Always look into your employer-sponsored retirement plan. Having a forced savings strategy is a great way to accumulate financial security.

APP #8
BUSINESS FOUNDATION

#Risingblackbusinessqueens

*"I had to make my own living and my
own opportunity. But I made it! Don't sit down and
wait for the opportunities to come.
Get up and make them."*

— Madam C.J. Walker

It is a great idea to learn about business at a young age. Business is constantly happening all around you. You may not think of cutting grass, shoveling snow, washing cars, trading sneakers or clothing as a business, but your interactions with others in the buying and selling of your services or trading products, are in fact conducting business.

Every day you are engaging in business when you are a paying customer of an organization. Of course, the companies you are likely doing business with are large corporations. However, chances are, these companies started off very small, and many leaders of these large corporations probably ran several small businesses before they became successful.

What is Business?

Business is really making a living buying and selling a product or service. If you decide to just go on your own based on a passion, you will wear the business label of "entrepreneur." An entrepreneur is a risk-taking business owner who undertakes an innovative business opportunity to bring the next best product or service to the global marketplace.

Owning a business is hard work. It takes a special amount of passion, dedication and determination to be successful. If business ownership is something you have thought about, do your research on the industry and your target market. It is also a great idea to try to get some experience in the field you want to invest your own product or service. There are several good business resources available from the Small Business

Administration that have partnered with other organizations to help you launch. The government encourages business ownership as it helps stimulate the economy with job creation. If it really makes you move on the inside, then go for it!

One of the biggest advantages you have in starting a business is the fact that you are technologically savvy. That means you know how to use the latest technology to spread your marketing and social media platform. All of the new apps and other internet tools have made doing business around the world a lot faster and easier.

In fact, you're never too young to start a business. There is no age limit for a great idea for a new product or service. Oftentimes, younger people are better positioned to see a need in the market, since you are more in tune with your peers and technology.

Being your own boss can be a lot cooler than being an employee, but remember that since you are starting out, you have to be flexible enough to wear a lot of hats; sales, advertising and marketing, website, customer service, and bookkeeping.

Are You A Good Fit?

The idea of being your own boss sounds great. You have no one to answer to or any worries about being fired. It's a huge responsibility. Can you handle it?

It takes a certain type of person to be at their best when no one is looking over their shoulder to clock in or out. As I mentioned earlier, you have to wear several hats every day and become good at a lot of things quickly.

One of the most challenging things for people is time management. How good are you at managing your time now? Are your assignments on time? Do you arrive early for work? Are family and friends constantly waiting for you to show up? Are you a procrastinator? If you have not exercised good time management habits, then starting your own business may not be right for you at this point in your life. Time management takes practice and is a learned process.

Another key personality trait that you need as a business owner is that you have to be a genuine go-getter. Customers are not just going to find you. You have to go out and get them. In addition, you have to know your market and be skilled enough to anticipate their needs and plan ahead. If you are going to succeed, you have to be self-motivated and prepared for the highs and lows with owning a business.

The key is to have a solid written business plan with realistic projections so you can withstand the ups and downs, and be able to revise the plan as needed. You will also need a detailed marketing plan to hone in on your target market. Most people want to skip the written plans because the idea is so great and customers are asking for the product or service right now. If you are serious about starting a business, be prepared for uncertainty. Your plan should have alternative strategies during challenging times and on those day where you have thoughts of quitting.

Business Ideas

What business ideas have been roaming around in your head? Have you researched it? Is it a product or service that you currently use? Do your homework and research the various opportunities for you to take your business to the marketplace. Consider the following examples below.

Online: The internet and online businesses are popping up by the thousands every day. That doesn't mean there isn't room for your product or service. There are many T-shirt manufacturers and other novelty and accessory manufacturers that allows you to create your own brand on their products and sell them on your website or through other channels like Amazon.

Drop shipping: This is also an online business where you can save money since you do not have to buy product inventory. Dropshipping companies charge you a monthly fee to be part of their service and you select the products in their inventory to sell on your own website. They handle all of the shipping and inventory on your behalf. You split the costs of each item you sell with the dropshipping company.

Craft: You can always make money off of your creativity. Whether you make novelty craft items, draw, paint, or design, you can always create your own website and sell your crafts. A popular website for creative people to sell their items is www.etsy.com.

Service: Are you a good writer? Researcher? Good with numbers? Good at organizing? Great communicator? If you have any skills that can help make a person's life easier by providing a service, then you should research the market and see how your unique service can be marketable.

The most important thing when starting a business is doing your research and having a written business plan to guide you through your daily activities.

INVESTING

Once you begin to see profits in your business, it is good idea to start learning about investing. Even if you don't have the extra money to do so, the sooner you understand the bigger picture of business success, the better prepared you will be when your next financial opportunity arises.

Stocks & Bonds

Our economy is built on business growth. As I mentioned earlier, both the state and federal government encourage small business ownership. Just like you are never too young to start a business, you are not too young to learn the basics of investing and how the stock market works. There are tons of resources to provide you with information, so please talk to your mentor or other advisor and do your research.

Keep in mind that investing is a risky business. The stock market will always be unpredictable. You could make a profit or you could lose a lot of money. Stocks tend to be more risky than bonds because they are relying on a corporation meeting or exceeding its projections. As with anything, no matter how much research and past history, unexpected things could go wrong. Bonds are less risky because they are usually backed (guaranteed) by the government and stable banks. They have a lower rate of return.

Many young people can get started in the market by using a technique called Dollar Cost Averaging (DCA). Using the DCA method you can buy a stock of a company for a set dollar amount regardless of the share price. This means you can buy more stock when the price is low and less when the price is high. Either way, you can set up bi-weekly or monthly purchase amounts for a company you believe in.

If there are companies that you are interested in purchasing shares, the first thing to do is to get a copy of their investors' package which should be available online. Keep in mind that there are fees for investing and fees to make transactions. Choose companies that you are familiar with and are already a purchaser of their product or service. You can track your stocks on your phone with various apps.

Regardless of where you are in your life, whether high school, college, recent college graduate, or currently employed, venturing into business is a great way to become financially stable and responsible. #Risingblackbusinessqueens.

Mirror, Mirror

Queen Mikaila Ulmer
Me & The Bees Lemonade

When she was only 10 years old, Mikaila Ulmer made an appearance on Shark Tank for her grandmother's flaxseed lemonade recipe. She was given $60,000 on the show for her lemonade. Today, she is thirteen and has her lemonade in Whole Foods and other markets.

Mikaila became fascinated with bees after being stung by them. She started researching and learned the importance of bees to our environment. Without, bees, we would die within a few years. That's when she decided to sweeten her lemonade with local honey instead of sugar. Today, she is on a mission to save bees and give back to those in need. Her slogan is "Buy a Bottle, Save the Bees!" Do you have a family recipe that you believe is marketable?

Queen's Wisdom

★ There will always be a need for new businesses to provide products and services. Research trends and find a niche to meet consumer demand.

★ Check out some of the youngest successful business owners and you will see that you are never too young to start a business.

★ You must have a strong work ethic to run a business as it requires you to take on several responsibilities.

★ Take a good look at your skills to determine if any of them can be the start of your income-earning business.

APP #9
Love and Relationship Foundation

#Practiceselflove

*"You've got to learn to
leave the table
when love is no longer
being served."*

— *Nina Simone*

Relationship Limits

"We give a lot of others significance in our lives even when they don't deserve it...If they're not good for you, they've got to go."

— **Gabrielle Union**

As a beautiful queen, you more than likely will be involved in romantic relationships. Of course there is nothing wrong with that, however, it is important to realize that in all healthy relationships, respect and communication are key factors in your overall well-being. It doesn't matter what your relationship status is: single, dating, casually dating, long term relationship, or "it's just complicated."

You must have an idea of where you stand in a relationship. What are your core values? Where do you look to meet guys? Online? At school? At work? At church? Check that guy out as much as you can before you send that first text or social media connect. Once you develop deep feelings and a connection to someone, it can be difficult to act with clear thinking as your heart may take over. Really be honest with yourself before that first kiss and think about what is too far or too much for you to be comfortable.

Are you Ready?

*"Let's talk about sex baby
Let's talk about you and me
Let's talk about all the good things
And the bad things that may be..."*

— **Salt-N-Pepa**

Sex is complicated regardless of your age. When it comes to sex, make sure you seriously consider how far you want to go when you are in a relationship. Know your limits before you get into an uncomfortable situation with a guy you really like. According to Emily Roberts, author of *Express Yourself,* when it comes to romantic relationships, you have the right to set your own boundaries. Yet when that moment is unexpected and you're feeling pressured or confused, it is easy to forget your personal rights.

A Queen's Rights

- You have the right to be treated with respect.
- You have the right to change your mind, to fall out of love, and live with no threats.
- You have the right not to be abused – physically, emotionally, or sexually.
- You have the right to say "no" to anything that makes you feel uncomfortable .
- You have the right to express your own opinions.
- You have the right to private time and your own space.
- You have the right to have friends of your own.
- You have the right to end any relationship.

Romantic relationships take our emotions to levels that we didn't even know existed. Being in and out of love can cause us to feel hurt, anxiety, stress and total distraction from our goals.

There is no easy fix to guarding our hearts, yet there are a few things to keep in mind as we move forward.

Love or Control

It can be extremely difficult to accept when you are in a unhealthy relationship. Your friends and family might have noticed it happening already and tried to talk to you about it, but you think they're totally wrong. Your boyfriend *loves* you so much that he wants to know your every move. That's not love. He wants to control you. Isn't that a sign that he cares? He just wants to spend more time with you or maybe wants more of your attention, right? Wrong. Consider talking to someone to help you steer clear of this relationship.

Oh the Games Women Play

Just as it is vitally important not to let jealousy become an issue in your relationship, it is also a huge mistake to play the type of games with your boyfriend that can result in jealousy.

The Break Up

Let's face it, many girls and women have experienced a break up. We have all been there or have heard stories of someone curled up in bed, crying as it were the end of the world. Even though the guy ended the relationship and even though you know it was the best thing for both of you, it still hurts like nothing else you have ever experienced. What would you do with yourself now? Would you ever fall in love again? Had you made a mistake in agreeing to the breakup? Should you call him and suggest that you try again? How are you going to make it through the rest of the day, let alone the rest of your life?

Breaking up is one of the most painful events anyone can go through, and for teens and young adults, who tend to be low on experience and high on emotion and hormones, it can be absolutely overwhelming.

Breakup Etiquette

When you're in the middle of a breakup, it can be hard to re-member to be kind and patient, but it is also vitally import-ant. In today's world of electronic communication, it can feel much easier to rely on texts, calls, and emails to deliver the bad news, and that is just what some teens do. Research conduct-ed by the Gravitate Research Group, who surveyed more than 4,000 people between the ages of 18 and 34 claims about 64% have argued with their significant other via text, and 39% of respondents ended a relationship with a message, not a call or in-person breakup. Another 55% would consider breaking up with someone with a text. The survey results stated, "When it comes to breaking up a relationship, many of the young people interviewed chose to send a text because that would make the conversation a lot less messy. There would be no eye contact, no tone of voice, no feeling awkward" (Murphy Nikelle, 2006).

Obviously, it feels less stressful to text. You don't have to see the tears of the hurt on your boyfriend's face and you won't be interrupted. Some people handle face-to-face tension or disagreement better than others. Many sensitive adolescents and teenagers like to avoid conflict and hurting others. They do not like to see the consequences of their actions, Texting also helps young people cope with the situation and allows them to move forward with ending the relationship.

The same is true for leaving a voicemail or sending an email or a private message via social media. It is somewhat cowardly and even disrespectful to break up in this manner, especially if the relationship was a close or intense one.

Feelings

Once the breakup is over, it's time to deal with the emotions it carries along with it. These feelings can be overwhelming and hard to cope with for many reasons. Whenever your feelings are hurt, it's helpful to stop and ask yourself this question: *How will I handle this*? Most of us let our emotions take over and we go with our knee-jerk reaction. If you are mad, you will yell. If you are frustrated, you vent. If you are sad or crushed, you withdraw, and refuse to face the world. Trust me, I've been there!

Letting your emotions control you however, is not the best solution. If your emotions go unchecked, it can cause tremendous damage and lead to your self-destruction or the destruction of other people's lives. Try not to internalize the hurt, because it will damage you in the long run. Your problems will not go away, they will only grow larger and spill over into other areas of your life. It takes practice to be in control of your situation. Self-control will lead to better decision-making in how you handle your hurt. Don't react out of emotion right away. Instead, wait until you are in a more rational state of mind before responding.

Road to Recovery

Sadly, there is no magic pill or single solution to getting over the pain of a break up. It takes time, often months to feel like you've gotten past it. In the meantime there are a number of ways to make you temporarily forget the pain.

Everyone experiences unhappy situations on occasion, but there is a big difference between having unhappiness periods and living an usual unhappy life. While there are some exceptions, most people's unhappiness stems in large part from self-neglect. Even if you are generally a happy go lucky person, neglecting yourself is something that can happen without you realizing it. The solution is to give yourself the extra attention you need and deserve. Ignoring your own feelings will not benefit you. It leads to emotional trauma, physical stress, behavior and mood changes, and yes...shattered relationships. When you routinely neglect yourself, your standards may plunge, and you may end up in a rebound relationship, making it harder to recover. Stop and ask yourself: "Do I love myself enough, including my needs, standards and wants, to make me my number one priority?" Find the strength to *"answer"*, Yes!

Life is about being a productive and good citizen. It's about doing the best thing for you, no matter what. When it's all said and done, your reputation is what other people know about you, so having a crazy moment in public when you let your emotions get the best of you can ruin your career. Always do a self-checkup and tap into your moral compass to maintain your honorable reputation. #Practiceselflove.

Mirror, Mirror

Self-Reflection

What To Look For In Relationships

As we have talked about, personal relationships can be challenging whether with our sister friends or romantic relationships. Unfortunately, many of the examples we have of relationships are what we see on television or in the movies. We also base our relationships on social media posts with hastags like #relatonshipshgoals. Yet, most of what we see is not realistic or totally false. Everyone wants to paint a public picture of a fairy tale experience with their perfect boo.

You need to base your relationships on y*our* personal values and not look at others. What is important to you in a relationship? What's on your wish list? Is it intelligence, kindness, reliability, maturity, communication or a sense of humor? All of these are important, and you will see a person's true character early on to know if the relationship will go forward. At the end of the day, since we are all unique with various life experiences, our needs in another person will differ. However, choosing someone with similar values, work ethic and goals will make for a happier relationship in the long run. #Practiceselflove.

Queen's Wisdom

★ Don't jump into romantic relationships too quickly. Allow the friendship to grow naturally before being exclusive.

★ Relationships tend to take us on emotional rollercoasters. Don't allow your emotions to control you in the event of a break up. Create a distance from the person to give you time to cool down and think about your response.

★ Choose a person who shares your values and meets a number of your "wish list" qualities in a mate.

★ Rebounding from a bad relationship takes time. Talk to a friend or a professional if you feel overwhelmed with thoughts of moving on.

APP #10
SOCIAL RESPONSIBILITY FOUNDATION

#Yourcommunityneedsyou

*"When you learn, teach.
When you get, give."*

— *Maya Angelou*

Paying it Forward

Helping others should be one of the most important character traits you possess. We were designed to use our gifts and talents to benefit others as well as ourselves. Life has a reciprocal principle—you get what you put out. Therefore, if you shift your mindset from selfishness and a "what's in it for me?" attitude, then more opportunities will arise for you.

A good way to get involved in paying it forward is to volunteer in your community. There are so many causes for you to be inspired to help. Find something that you are passionate about like a healthier community, safety, after-school programs (activities and academics), teen support groups, anti-bullying, the elderly and the environment are just a few examples.

Volunteering gives you a chance to share your skills with others, as well as practice your communication, organization, and leadership skills. You may be fortunate and learn a new area of community service or business. All of the roles and responsibilities you perform while volunteering can be highlighted on your resume and college applications.

The satisfaction that you feel when you lend a hand to help others cannot be monetized. As you further your career, you will see the benefit of reaching back as a mentor, event organizer or donor. There are so many athletes, celebrities, and leaders, who donate their time and money throughout the year for causes they believe in. Even though you may just be starting out, your efforts are just as valuable as someone more experienced and well-known.

I've found that it can be difficult for young people to envision helping others because they may not have experienced anyone helping them. That's why it is important to step outside of your comfort zone, see how others are living, in order to help shape your views about your future, and what you have to offer.

Have you ever heard about some problem or injustice and thought, *"I wish there were something I could do about that?"* Well most likely there is. Concerned and committed young people are working around the world for a better future, and you can too. Check out the Resources section to see how and where you can help. #Yourcommunityneedsyou.

Mirror, Mirror

Queen Emma Gonzalez Parkland Student Survivor Gun Control Activist

On February 14, 2018, 17 students and teachers were senselessly gunned down by a former student at Marjory Stoneman Douglas (MSD) High School in Parkland, Florida. There were also 17 injuries in what has been the deadliest high school shooting to date. Since then, students of MSD have banned together to lend their voice and actions to gun reform with their **Never Again** campaign to urge politicians for gun reform. Amongst the most outspoken is the intelligent, Emma Gonzalez.

Emma has become an activist and advocate for gun control. She was a senior at MSD when the mass shooting occurred. Immediately after this tragedy, Emma and her classmates began organizing the March for Our Lives on Washington DC a few weeks later. She made a powerful and emotional speech during the March for Our Lives for six minutes, which was the amount of time the gunman used to kill her friends and teachers. She also honored the victims and continues to speak out on gun control.

Since then, Florida Governor Rick Scott signed a Bill that raised the minimum age for buying a rifle from 18 to 21. The Bill also put waiting periods in place for gun purchases, allowed for the arming of teachers, disallowed bump stocks to make firing easier, and most important, disallowed mentally unstable people to purchase guns. Emma Gonzalez is a true queen doing her part to make all of our lives safer. What can you do to make a difference to help others?

Queen's Wisdom

★ You will find happiness and a sense of fulfillment when you pay it forward and help others.

★ Life is about reciprocity; you get back what you give. Be kind and seek to give.

★ Making a positive impact in the lives of others can do more for your future success than anything you can do on your own.

★ Loving and caring for someone other than yourself is one of the reasons that you were created.

★ Always look to help first. Whether it is through service, providing a solution to a problem or connecting others, having a humble, helpful, spirit will unlock doors and unleash opportunities that you never knew existed.

Final Thoughts

#MeTooMovement

In 2006, Tarana Burke coined the phrase "Me Too" as a way to help women who had survived sexual violence. Fast-forward more than 10 years, and the phrase has been reignited as the slogan of the anti-sexual harassment movement. A movement that has rocked some of the most powerful men in entertainment and politics. A movement whose timeline continues to rapidly build.

Last year, hundreds of women across the country liberated themselves through the hashtag #MeToo, in which survivors of sexual harassment and assault came forward on social media. The movement, ignited by Hollywood, quickly spread to the White House. However, there's a group of women in particular that are afraid to speak up: undocumented immigrants.

In the wake of the 2018 #TimesUp movement, an unified call was initiated by women in entertainment that pushed for changes to turn workplaces into a safe and equitable place for all women. Yet for all the awareness and good that the #MeToo-Movement has ignited, the application of its exposure has not been applied equally to Black women.

For example, in April, 2018, a 25-year-old Black woman named Chikesia Clemons was arrested with such brutal force by police at a Waffle House restaurant in Alabama, as if she were a criminal on a Most Wanted poster. In fact, all Ms. Clemons wanted was for the restaurant to provide her with plastic utensils as the silverware she was given was dirty.

Fortunately, a video of the arrest immediately went viral that shows two Alabama police officers pulling Clemons from her chair and throwing her to the floor which caused her breasts to be exposed. As she attempts to cover her breasts, the officers threaten to break her arm for "resisting".

Although Ms. Clemons' experience with the police is tragic, it is not unique. In the U.S., Black women have historically not been granted the same regard for our bodily privacy as white women. From our impregnation by our slave masters, to strip and cavity searches in public by police departments all over the country, our bodies have been on full display.

While I applaud the success of the#MeTooMovement in exposing high profile males, I am saddened and frustrated that it does not apply to us in the same manner as it does to white women, even though a Black woman, Tarana Burke created the campaign in the first place. If positive women's movements like #MeToo are really concerned about fighting sexual violence in the workplace and in general, then they have to also include women of color and Latina immigrants.

Bonus: Queen's Wisdom

Here is more wisdom from women who have been in your shoes that you can learn from to help you along your journey. Take the time to read them and hopefully these words will connect with you.

"Whenever I feel bad, I use that feeling to motivate me to work harder. I only allow myself one day to feel sorry for myself. When I'm not feeling my best I ask myself, 'What are you gonna do about it?' I use the negativity to fuel the transformation into a better me."

— *Beyoncé*

"A great figure or physique is nice, but it's self-confidence that makes someone really sexy."

— *Vivica Foxx*

"Wanna fly, you got to give up the shit that weighs you down."

— *Toni Morrison*

"I used to want the words "She tried" on my tombstone. Now I want "She did it.""

— *Katherine Dunham*

"Being a woman of curves, I really find that it's very important to talk about loving your body where you are."

— *Danielle Brooks*

"You can't just sit there and wait for people to give you that golden dream. You've got to get out there and make it happen for yourself."

— *Diana Ross*

"Women need to celebrate their God-given beauty instead of always trying to be something else."

— *Iman*

To be a queen of a household is a powerful thing.

— *Jill Scott*

"If it is easy, then you are doing it wrong."

— *Gabby Williams*

"I'm convinced that we Black women possess a special indestructible strength that allows us to not only get down, but to get up, to get through, and to get over."

— *Janet Jackson*

"The only thing that separates women of color from anyone else is opportunity."

— *Viola Davis*

"It doesn't matter what your background is and where you come from, if you have dreams and goals, that's all that matters."

— *Serena Williams*

"Some people say I have attitude - maybe I do... but I think you have to. You have to believe in yourself when no one else does - that makes you a winner right there."

— *Venus Williams*

Extra Bonus: King's Wisdom

Whether impactful advice comes from a male or female, it is bound to have a positive impact on your future. Take note of some of the empowering quotes from many outstanding men trailblazers of recent years.

"Greatness is not this wonderful, esoteric, elusive, God-like, feature that only the special among us will ever taste. It's something that truly exists in all of us. It's very simple. This is what I believe, and I'm willing to die for it."

— *Will Smith*

"Belief in oneself and knowing who you are, I mean, that's the foundation for everything great."

— *Jay Z*

"Obstacles don't have to stop you. If you run into a wall, don't turn around and give up. Figure out how to climb it, go through it, or work around it."

— *Michael Jordan*

"I just come do what I've got to do, play my game. And I don't worry if anybody likes it."

— *David Ortiz*

"I'm going to use all my tools, my God-given ability, and make the best life I can with it."

— *LeBron James*

"My Vocation is my Vacation. I love what I do."

— *Nick Cannon*

"Keep going. No matter what."

— *Reginald Lewis*

"Life is a menu so remember whoever and whatever you order for your life is what's gonna be delivered to your table."

— *Tyrese*

"Don't be afraid to be ambitious about your goals. Hard work never stops. Neither should your dreams."

— *Dwayne "The Rock" Johnson*

"If you're going to do something, you're going to do it to be the best."

— *Colin Kaepernick*

"I believe in destiny. But I also believe that you can't just sit back and let destiny happen. A lot of times, an opportunity might fall into your lap, but you have to be ready for that opportunity. You can't sit there waiting on it. A lot of times you are going to have to get out there and make it happen."

— *Spike Lee*

"My mother used to tell me, man gives the award, God gives the reward. I don't need another plaque."

— *Denzel Washington*

"I never thought of losing, but now that it's happened, the only thing is to do it right. That's my obligation to all the people who believe in me. We all have to take defeats in life."

— *Muhammad Ali*

"Nothing in this world is more POWERFUL than Colored Women!!"

— *LeBron James*

Royal Affirmations

Weekly Planner

Monday

Tuesday

Wednesday

Thursday

Friday

Saturday

Sunday

Don't Forgot!

To Do:

Take Notes!

References/Notes

Amay, J. and articles..., R. (2018). *10 Best Black Beauty Bloggers We're Obsessed With - theFashionSpot.* [online] theFashionSpot. Available at: http://www.thefashionspot.com/beauty/586905-10-best-black-beauty-bloggers/#/slide/1 [Accessed 14 Aug. 2018].

Anon, (2018). [online] Available at: https://datacenter.kidscount.org/data/tables/107-children-in-single-parent-families-by#detailed/1/any/false/870,573,869,36,868/10,11,9,12,1,185,13/432,431 [Accessed 14 Aug. 2018].

Anon, (2018). [online] Available at: https://www.usnews.com/news/education-news/articles/2017-05-09/black-girls-are-twice-as-likely-to-be-suspended-in-every-state [Accessed 14 Aug. 2018].

Bedard, Paul, and Seth Wenig. "77% Black Births to Single Moms, 49% for Hispanic Immigrants." *Washington Examiner*, 5 May 2017, www.washingtonexaminer.com/77-black-births-to-single-moms-49-for-hispanic-immigrants#!

Blacklosangeles.wordpress.com/2011/05/03/the-effects-of-single-mother-families-on-children-in-an-african-american-household/.

Brenner, G. (2018). *Silence, Stillness, and the Art of Being.* [online] Dr. Gail Brenner. Available at: http://gailbrenner.com/2011/11/silence-stillness-and-the-art-of-being/ [Accessed 14 Aug. 2018].

Cdc.gov. (2018). *African Americans | Race/Ethnicity | HIV by Group | HIV/AIDS | CDC.* [online] Available at: https://www.cdc.gov/hiv/group/racialethnic/africanamericans/index.html [Accessed 14 Aug. 2018].

Chernoff, Marc, and Angel Chernoff. *Getting Back to Happy: Change Your Thoughts, Change Your Reality, and Turn Your Trials into Triumphs.* TarcherPerigee, 2018.

Chicago Tribune. "#MeToo Today: How the Movement Has Evolved since the Initial Weinstein Allegations." *Chicagotribune.com*, 14 June 2018, www.chicagotribune.com/lifestyles/ct-metoo-20171218-story.html.

"ChicagoTribune-WeAreCurrentlyUnavailableInYourRegion". *Chicagotribune. Com*, 2018, http://www.chicagotribune.com/lifestyles/ct-me-too-timeline-20171208-htmlstory.html. Accessed 14 Aug 2018.

Childwelfare.gov. (2018). [online] Available at: https://www.childwelfare. gov/pubPDFs/foster.pdf [Accessed 14 Aug. 2018].

Essence. (2018). *New Study Shows Black Women Are Among Most Educated In U.S. | [site:name]*. [online] Available at: https://www.essence.com/news/ new-study-black-women-most-educated/ [Accessed 14 Aug. 2018].

INSIDER. (2018). *Everything you need to know about Barack and Michelle Obama's love story — from the law office to the Oval Office*. [online] Available at: https://www.thisisinsider.com/how-did-barack-and-michelle-obama-meet-2017-10 [Accessed 14 Aug. 2018].

Johnson, Greta Hendricks. "African American Sororities." Carnegie, Andrew | Learning to Give, www.learningtogive.org/resources/african-american-sororities.

Kampakis, Kari. *Liked: Whose Approval Are You Living For?* 2016..

Matthews, S. (n.d.). *The effects of the father-son relationship: A qualitative study*.

Nikelle-Snader. "55% Of Young People Would Break Up Via Text: Would You?" *The Cheat Sheet*, The Cheat Sheet, 6 Jan. 2016, www.cheatsheet. com/health-fitness/55-of-young-people-would-break-up-via-text-would-you.html/?a=viewall.

Me, About et al. "How To Slay These Fashions While Saving Them Coins". *Lisa A La Mode*, 2018, https://lisaalamode.com/2017/08/19/how-to-maximize-your-wardrobe/. Accessed 14 Aug 2018.

Roberts, Emily, and Jennifer L. Hartstein. *Express Yourself A Teen Girls Guide to Speaking up and Being Who You Are*. New Harbinger Publications, 2015.

Reporters, T. (2018). *Mark Zuckerberg finally gets his Harvard degree - 12 years after dropping out*. [online] The Telegraph. Available at: https://www. telegraph.co.uk/technology/2017/05/25/mark-zuckerberg-finally-gets-harvard-degree-12-years-dropping/ [Accessed 14 Aug. 2018].

"Skin Cancer Facts & Statistics - Skincancer.Org". *Skincancer.Org*, 2018, https://www.skincancer.org/skin-cancer-information/skin-cancer-facts. Accessed 14 Aug 2018.

"Sorority Life." *Sorority Life*, www.thesororitylife.com/newsdetail.aspx?id=96.

"State Of African-American Children In Foster Care | Foster Care Advocates | Foster Coalition". *Foster Care Advocates | Foster Coalition*, 2018, http://www.fostercoalition.com/single-post/2015/02/27/State-of-AfricanAmerican-Children-in-Foster-Care. Accessed 14 Aug 2018.

Teen Dating Bill of Rights. (n.d.). Retrieved from http://respect2all.org/teen-dating-bill-of-rights/

"The Divine Nine and the National Pan-Hellenic Council." *Black Greeks - Black Greek.com,* www.blackgreek.com/index.html.

"The Effects of Single-Mother Families on Children in an African-American Household." *BLACK LOS ANGELES*, 3 May 2011,

"The Vanishing Family: Crisis In Black America | Billmoyers.Com". *Billmoyers. Com*, 2018, https://billmoyers.com/content/the-vanishing-family-crisis-in-black-. Accessed 14 Aug 2018.

10 Ultimate Truths Girls Should Know. Paw Prints, 2014.

"13 Mental Health Benefits Of Exercise". *Huffpost*, 2018, https://www.huffingtonpost.com/2013/03/27/mental-health-benefits-exercise_n_2956099.html. Accessed 14 Aug 2018.

2018, https://datacenter.kidscount.org/data/tables/107-children-in-single-parent-families-by#detailed/1/any/false/870,573,869,36,868/10,11,9,12,1,185,13/432,431. Accessed 14 Aug2018.

A List of Clubs & Organizations That Empower Black Girls

Above &Beyond Initiative

This foundation is designed for the youth to be part of a program that provides peer support and hope through discussions and activities and service projects. It is designed to educate youth on how to deal with the complex situations they face day to day.

ABI is a New York City based nonprofit leadership organization that aim to serve African American teenage girls from the 9th to 12th grade. Through rigorous hands-on workshops, programs, activities and discussions, ABI strives to develop the skills necessary to excel as professional women and produce a new wave of confidence that will be successfully integrated into society.

For more on the organization and how to get involved, visit http://aboveandbeyondini.org

Afro Puffs and Ponytails, Inc.

Afro Puffs and Ponytails, Inc. is a non-profit organization created primarily for supporting and uplifting African American/Black

Girls! Our website provides encouraging articles, events, program listings, and resources for African American/Black teen girls, young girls, and their parents.

Purpose

To inspire and recognize success in African American young girls and teen girls

Mission

To seek to empower African American young girls and teen girls by teaching the importance of taking care of the mind, body, and spirit.

Aim

- To encourage African American girls to pursue education and knowledge
- To help African American Girls learn to appreciate and embrace their unique beauty, inside and out
- To build confidence and a strong sense of self worth
- We seek to accomplish this important endeavor by:
- Promoting and reinforcing positive actions and behaviors
- Publishing helpful articles and resources
- Providing bio's about successful African American women
- Planting and nurturing seeds for success

For more on the organization and how to get involved, visit https://afropuffsandponytails.com

Akili Dada Institute (Nairobi, Kenya)

Akili Dada is an organization that develops girls in Kenya through an "incubator leadership program." The organization takes a "holistic approach to leadership development, providing wrap around support, including financial support, mentorship, skills training, leadership development and platforms for girls and young women to share their stories, ideas, challenges and innovations." One of the interesting things about this organization is its young change makers program that is offered to teenage girls to develop as leaders within their various communities, particularly their schools. The program includes offering scholarships to girls and providing in-school activities for the girls as well as mentorship and other opportunities. For more on the organization and how to get involved, visit AKILIDADA.org or Instagram @Akilidada.

Black Girl Codes

Black Girls CODE is devoted to showing the world that black girls can code, and do so much more. By reaching out to the community through workshops and after school programs, Black Girls CODE introduces computer coding lessons to young girls from underrepresented communities in programming languages such as Scratch or Ruby on Rails. Black Girls CODE has set out to prove to the world that girls of every color have the skills to become the programmers of tomorrow. By promoting classes and programs we hope to grow the number of women of color working in technology and give underprivileged girls a chance to become the masters of their technological worlds. Black Girls CODE's ultimate goal is to provide African-American youth with the skills to occupy some of the 1.4 million computing job openings expected to be available in the U.S. by 2020, and to train 1 million girls by 2040.

For more on the organization and how to get involved, visit http://www.blackgirlscode.com

Black Girls Rock, Inc.

The mission of BLACK GIRLS ROCK! is to change the world by empowering Black girls to lead, innovate, and serve. BLACK GIRLS ROCK!™ Inc., is a 501(c)(3) nonprofit organization, that has been committed to enriching girls through leadership, education, and positive identity development since 2006. BLACK GIRLS ROCK!™ Inc. builds the self-esteem and self-worth of young women of color by changing their outlook on life, broadening their horizons and providing tools for self-empowerment and efficacy. *Founded by celebrity DJ and philanthropist, Beverly Bond, BLACK GIRLS ROCK!™ is also a multifaceted movement dedicated to shifting the cultural paradigms of media/music messaging that often negatively impact women and girls. For more on the organization and how to get involved, http://www.blackgirlsrockinc.com*

Black Girls Smile Inc.

Black Girls Smile Inc. was founded in 2012 by Lauren Carson based on the gaps she found throughout her mental health journey as a young African American female with clinical depression. Lauren envisioned a society that through the normalization and dialogue surrounding mental wellness, all individuals, including young African American females would be provided the education, support and resources necessary to lead a positively mentally healthy life. Black Girls Smile Inc. was born!

BGS actively engages participants in educational activities to promote mental health education and awareness.

Individual program workshops range from one day, 3 days, or eight to twelve weeks.

Most BGS programs can be customized extending to three, six and nine months on-going programs.

Program workshop presentations and materials are tailored to be developmentally appropriate for the participating age groups.

When focusing on sensitive topics surrounding mental health our utmost concern is ensuring a safe, non-judgmental and confidential environment.

For more on the organization and how to get involved, visit http://www.blackgirlssmile.org

Brown Girl Magic

Brown Girl Magic was created by 12-year-old aspiring actress and student Mikaela Sydney Smith who started the organization after creating Mikaela's "Crazy Knee Socks for a Cause" campaign to collect socks for kids in need during the winter season. Mikaela was inspired after reading the book, "Chicken Soup for the Preteen Soul" and just like the heroic teens outlined in the book, Mikaela decided to extend her charitable services to brown girls like herself and develop a conference to empower and charge all brown girls to realize their inner magic to make a difference in their communities. Mikaela is also a budding actress and being a brown girl with natural hair and curves, she has witnessed firsthand at her young age, the negativity resulting from mainstream not valuing her beauty inside and out. Still Mikaela strives to make a difference and plans to take the world by storm by holding a conference and inviting her Brown Girl Magic Ambassadors from across the globe to join her on a day filled with inspiration from powerful speakers.

For more on the organization and how to get involved, visit http://www.browngirlmagic.com/about-us.html

Brown Girls Do Ballet

First founded as an avenue to highlight more young people of color in the arts, Brown Girls Do Ballet, a part of 'Brown Girls Do,' is a community that provides scholarships, mentoring, and resources for young women of color. Their mission is to 'increase the participation of underrepresented minority populations in ballet programs through organizing and arranging performances, photo exhibitions, and providing resources and scholarships to assist young girls in their ballet development and training' according to their site.

Co-Founder TaKiyah Wallace searched her neighborhood for programs but could not find programs where her daughter would be the only brown face. In efforts to highlight diversity in dance, she former ballerina and media professional Brittani started the Brown Girls Do Instagram page which has grown into a movement. They sell products, have a photo exhibition, mentoring and ambassadors program, a directory where parents and caretakers can find 'Brown girl friendly' dance studios and more.

For more on the organization and how to get involved, visit https://www.browngirlsdoballet.com

Girl Effect

Experts in media, mobile, brand and international development. Founded by the Nike Foundation in 2004, today they are an independent creative non-profit working from nine global locations and active in 66 countries.

Through Girl Effect's work, a girl can start to express herself, value herself, and build the relationships she needs. In tangible, measurable ways. When she has the widespread belief and support of others, and when there are millions of girls like her, these changes become a new normal. Where she can seek out the things she needs – from vaccination to education to economic opportunity.

For more on the organization and how to get involved, visit https://www.girleffect.org

Girls For A Change

Girls For A Change devotes its energy and focus to the empowerment and uplifting of Black girls, and other girls of color. In part this decision was made because we, as an organization and movement, view this action as a first step to end the prejudice, poverty, and lack of resources that leave Black girls and women vulnerable at the margins of society.

We have chosen to focus on Black girls now both because of our understanding of current conditions via data and the presence of the persistent and widespread notion that women and girls of color in the United States are doing fine.(Shifman, Novo Foundation) Girls of color, specifically, black girls are at the margins of the mainstream community's concerns with respect to achievement gaps, the dropout crisis, and the school-to-prison pipeline.

Girls For A Change has develop gender and race-conscious prisms that address the vulnerabilities our girls experience today while advancing their 21st Century skills beyond the classroom. Girls For A Change works to ensure that we close opportunity gaps faced by too many disadvantaged, marginalized, or underrepresented girls—specifically black girls and ensure that they are ahead of the learning curve and will continue to inspire our partners to do the same—to ensure that every girls who aspires to get ahead has a chance to be seen, heard, celebrated and succeed.

For more on the organization and how to get involved, visit http://www.girlsforachange.org

Girls Going Global

The reason why this organization is so fantastic is that it exposes girls to traveling at such early ages! The organization describes itself as "a social enterprise aiming to expose African-American girls to the cultures of the world." Being that we live in a global world and the importance of Black girls getting to know the world around them beyond the classroom, this organization could not have come at a better time. The organization seeks to make young people "international game changers," particularly African-American girls who don't have access to such programs. The organization seeks to empower Black girls to become more knowledgeable of the world around them and diligent in matters of foreign affairs. With their long-term goal being empowering girls through travel, we applaud them for their efforts!

For more on the organization and how to get involved, visit http://www.girlsgoingglobal.org

Girls; Live, Love, Laugh Inc.

Girls; Live, Love, Laugh Inc. mission is to permit every girl between the ages of 6-16 years old in the city of Newark and neighboring communities a chance to live, love, and laugh out loud through our core workshops on leadership & career development, education, communications, health & wellness, bully prevention, time management & civic engagement.

The purpose of Girls; Live, Love, Laugh Inc. Is to make a difference in the lives of girls by removing some of the obstacles that may stand in their way, so that the can become respectable, successful, productive and happy ladies in society.

Girls; Live, Love, Laugh, Inc. implements a variety of programs for the young ladies in this organization that focuses on many pressing issues that are relevant in today's society.

For more on the organization and how to get involved, http://girlslivelovelaugh.org

God's Gift, Inc.

Established in 2009, God's Gift, Inc. is a 501c3 nonprofit organization that caters to girls 7-17 by providing career and college prep, life skills training, peer to peer mentoring, etiquette classes, self-esteem workshops, and leadership training and character building. Currently they operate out of Roosevelt Gardens Park in Fort Lauderdale, FL. . God's Gift, Inc. has host three afterschool programs, three summer camps, and a bi-weekly weekend mentoring program. We also offer a scholarship for graduating seniors entitled, "Women of Self Worth" scholarship. Many of the young ladies in this program are referred from schools, behavioral health centers and the Department of Juvenile Justice.

For more on the organization and how to get involved, visit http://wordpress.godsgiftinc.org

I Am A Girl Barbados (Barbados)

I Am a Girl Barbados focuses on working with girls in Barbados. A member-based organization, it has a strong focus on empowering girls to "create a positive change within themselves, their families and, by extension, their communities." The organization focuses on issues such as body image and self-esteem, domestic violence and many other issues relevant to the needs of girls in Barbados. I am a Girl Barbados "envisions a Barbadian Community where girls of every variety of background are fully afforded with the equal opportunities of education, employment, health care, safety and the chance to be positioned as the future leaders of region and the Caribbean." For more on the organization and how to get involved, visit I Am a Girl Barbados or Instagram @Iamagirlbarbados.

I Am Beautiful

Am B.E.A.U.T.I.F.U.L.™ is a thriving non-profit organization that engages girls in interactive learning experiences designed to build self-esteem and strong leadership skills to help girls and women live B.E.A.U.T.I.F.U.L. lives inside and out.

Our B.E.A.U.T.I.F.U.L. has little to do with lipstick and expensive wardrobe. Instead, we focus on building self-esteem and awareness by shifting the typical paradigm and teaching girls and women that what they have inside makes them beautiful, special and unique. B.E.A.U.T.I.F.U.L. is an acrostic meaning Brave, Energetic, Assertive, Unique, Tenacious, Important, Fabulous, Unequaled and Loved.

For more on the organization and how to get involved, visit http://www.iambeautiful.org

Island Girls Roc (Jamaica)

Founded by women from Jamaica, Island Girls Ruling Our Course is a nonprofit organization that works on enhancing the leadership skills of girls through a transformative leadership approach. The organization "empowers girls using education and creating opportunities for them to participate in activities of interest that ignite hope, inspires passion and assists them in creating a platform for their future." The organization uses technology and education as its main method to engage girls in Jamaica. Their goal is to create experiences for young girls to enable them to gain more "ownership and create direction for their future whilst increasing self-esteem."

For more on the organization and how to get involved, visit Islandgirlsroc.org.

Jelani Girls

Jelani Girls, Inc. is a labor of love birthed by the passion of our founder, Ashley Company. Recognizing a need for under-served girls to overcome the cyclical limitations of their social economic backgrounds, Ashley became steadfast in her pursuit of providing these young women with an opportunity to look beyond their backyards. Aware that there are different approaches to grow and develop these young women as well-rounded citizens and leaders in the community, Ashley conceptualized an organization that empowers young women to achieve greatness through full immersion in our Cultural Enrichment Program (CEP) and International Youth Service Project (IYSP).

For more on the organization and how to get involved, visit http://jelanigirls.org

Pearl for Teen Girls

PEARLS for Teen Girls is improving quality of life and strengthening our community one girl at a time by empowering young women with self-development tools, guidance and support to strive for better, brighter futures by living out the PEARLS values: Personal Responsibility, Empathy, Awareness, Respect, Leadership and Support.

PEARLS is rapidly becoming known among girls, funders and public and private entities in our community as "the program" for girls' self-development. Our programs provide girls with a safe place, skill development and self-esteem building that lead to better life choices and an opportunity to realize their full potential.

For more on the organization and how to get involved, visit https://www.pearlsforteengirls.com

Petals and Belles

We all know how important it is to influence the lives of girls living in any city, particularly girls of color. Petals and Belles founder Damali Elliot founded the organization to create a space for girls to receive support to become successful in life. The organization prides itself in its "multi-faceted approach" to empower the growth of girls, which includes workshops and after school, weekend and summer programs. One of the intriguing things about this organization is its mentorship program where young women are matched to the girls during their workshops. The organization's "innovative curriculum combines mentoring, creative workshops, awe-inspiringsocial experiences and academic coaching to ensure the SUCCESS of GIRLS."

For more on the organization and how to get involved, http://petalsnbelles.org

Pretty Brown Girl

Founded in 2010 as a unique, empowering self-esteem product line for girls, the Pretty Brown Girl Brand and Movement sends a simple, yet powerful message of self-love to girls and women everywhere. Our mission is to encourage self-acceptance by cultivating social, emotional and intellectual well-being.

Today, the Pretty Brown Girl Movement is ranked by NBC News as one of the top seven organizations dedicated to empowering girls and has expanded to offer engaging programs, clubs and events for girls. Over the past seven years, we have helped thousands of girls across the country to have increased self-esteem.

Pretty Brown Girl ensures it stays responsive to community needs in the same way it began, by listening to the voice of the girls and young women in which it serves. Our vision is to create a Pretty Brown Girl Movement designed to instill self-confidence, pride and leadership skills in young girls and young women of color to help propel them into their positions of power and community activism, thereby creating contributing women in society. We are working in communities daily, encouraging girls to reach for the stars and focus on their gifts, talents and education that can be used to elevate humanity.

For more on the organization and how to get involved, visit https://prettybrowngirl.com

Project Butterfly

Project Butterfly New Orleans (PBNOLA) has been in existence since January of 2009 and uses the Project Butterfly curriculum and other evidence-based youth development strategies to address key issues impacting the development of girls of African descent. PBNOLA frequently uses media, creative and performing arts, entrepreneurship, yoga, meditation, and other creative formats to engage girls on these issues. The program currently supports girls in grades 9-12 with plans to expand to serve girls in grades 6-12.

Project Butterfly is a nationally-recognized curriculum developed by Niambi Jaha Echols that is designed to assist girls of

African descent in their transition from adolescence to adulthood. This curriculum addresses girls' personal development and self-esteem as well as topics such as the influence of media on girls and women, body image, girls' health, effective decision-making, spirituality, and many other topics relevant to adolescent girls.

For more on the organization and how to get involved, http://www.projectbutterflynola.org

The Black Doll Affair

In 2005, in an attempt to "brown the playing field" in product marketing, Dana "Mama Doll" Hill had the chutzpah to create a self-promoting campaign (Got Spokesmodel?) and post a self-image billboard at the corners of 52nd Street and Broadway in New York's Times Square. The striking model and publicist at the time, received the rude awakening that she was the "black doll" that nobody was choosing.

In 2007, she founded The Black Doll Affair (TBDA), a philanthropic organization and self-esteem movement for black girls and women (The Black Dolls) to re-establish their self-esteem, self-image and worth in a society where black women are all too often lowest on the totem pole. TBDA is a solution to the infamous Doll Tests from the documentary 'A Girl Like Me' where black children associated black dolls with being "bad" and "ugly" and made it clear that they preferred white dolls, which they deemed "pretty" and "good." "The Black Doll Affair is not about the color of your skin. It's about loving the color of your skin, no matter what shade of black. It's about self-esteem in hue. It's about feeling good the way you were born – dark or light. It's about girls and women conquering self-defeating, self-limiting thought patterns of 'I'm not good enough because I was born a black girl. It's about loving who you are, and rejecting that pop culture statement: 'You're so pretty to be black!' " proclaims Hill.

For more on the organization and how to get involved, visit https://www.blackdollaffair.com/pages/founder

The Girls Education Initiative of Ghana (Ghana)

With the need for girls to receive additional education support and programming in Ghana, the organization Girls Education Initiative of Ghana was formed. The Girls Education Initiative of Ghana "provides academic and financial support for girls and applicants with special needs so that they can access higher education and professional opportunities." For more on the organization and how to get involved, visit GEIG GHANA or Instagram @GirlsEdGH.

Think Young Women (Gambia, West Africa)

Think Young Women (TYW) is an organization led by young African women activists in Gambia. The organization focuses on raising awareness on very controversial issues impacting young girls in Gambia including violence against women and in particular provides programming and awareness around harmful traditional practices such as FGM/C (Female Genital Mutilation/Cutting).

The organization is based on "the belief that young women and girls are active members of the wider community and play a vital role in it." In particular the organization seeks to create a community to empower and uplift young women in their society. For more on the organization and how to get involved, visit Think Young Women or Instagram @ThinkYoungWomen.

Uniquely You Summit

Based in Philadelphia, Uniquely You Summit has the aim to empower Black girls "where they are to go places they've never been." Recently the organization launched its #WhatIknownow campaign, a platform for Black women to provide advice to Black girls about life, career etc. This movement has become a space to bring different people together to also fundraise for the organization whilst spreading love to Black girls. Follow their Instagram account @UniquelyYusummit to get so much life and Black girl inspiration. For more on the organization and how to get involved visit Uniquelyyousummit.org.

Historically Black Greek Sororities

Alpha Kappa Alpha Sorority, Founded 1908, Howard University

Alpha Kappa Alpha Sorority, Inc. (AKA) is the first Greek letter organization in the United States established by Black college women. Established January 15, 1908 at Howard University, the organization has now grown to a membership of over 170,000, with graduate and undergraduate chapters representing every state and several foreign countries.

According to the official web site, "Alpha Kappa Alpha is a sisterhood composed of women who have consciously chosen this affiliation as a means of self-fulfillment through volunteer service. Alpha Kappa Alpha cultivates and encourages high scholastic and ethical standards; promotes unity and friendship among college women; alleviates problems concerning girls and women; maintains a progressive interest in college life; and serves all mankind..."

Delta Sigma Theta Sorority, Founded 1913, Howard University

Delta Sigma Theta Sorority was founded on January 13, 1913 by twenty-two collegiate women at Howard University. These students wanted to use their collective strength to promote academic excellence and to provide assistance to persons in need. The first public act performed by the Delta Founders involved their participation in the Women's Suffrage March in Washington D.C., March 1913. Delta Sigma Theta was incorporated in 1930.

According to the official web site, "The Grand Chapter of Delta Sigma Theta Sorority, Inc. has a membership of over 200,000 predominately African-American, college-educated women. The Sorority currently has 900-plus chapters located in the United States, Tokyo, Japan, Okinawa, Japan, Germany, Bermuda, the Bahamas, Seoul, Korea, and St. Thomas and St Croix in the U.S. Virgin Islands."

Zeta Phi Beta Sorority, Founded 1920, Howard University

Zeta Phi Beta Sorority was founded on the simple belief that sorority elitism and socializing should not overshadow the real mission for progressive organizations - to address societal and health concerns of the day. Founded January 16, 1920, Zeta began as an idea conceived by five coeds at Howard University in Washington D.C.

According to the official web site, "The purpose of Zeta Phi Beta Sorority is to foster the ideas of service, charity, scholarship, civil and cultural endeavors, sisterhood and finer womanhood. These ideals are reflected in the sorority's national program for which its members and auxiliary groups provide voluntary service to staff, community outreach programs, fund scholarships, support organized charities, and promote legislation for social and civic change."

Sigma Gamma Rho Sorority, Founded 1922, Butler University

Sigma Gamma Rho Sorority, Inc. was organized on November 12, 1922 in Indianapolis, Indiana by seven school teachers. The group became an incorporated national collegiate sorority on December 30, 1929.

According to the official web site, "Sigma Gamma Rho Sorority's aim is to enhance the quality of life within the community. Public service, leadership development and education of youth are the hallmark of the organization's programs and activities. Sigma Gamma Rho addresses concerns that impact society educationally, civically, and economically."

Famous African-American Sorority Members

Maya Angelou- Mrs. Angelou joined Alpha Kappa Alpha, the nation's first African-American sorority, in 1983 as an honorary member.

Angela Bassett- is a proud member of Delta Sigma Theta Sorority, Inc.

Towanda Braxton- Towanda is a proud member of Zeta Phi Beta sorority, Inc.

Natalie Cole- The late multiple Grammy-winning recording artist Natalie Cole is a member of Delta Sigma Theta Sorority, Inc.

Ruby Dee- is a proud member of Delta Sigma Theta Sorority, Inc.

Loretta Devine- Loretta was initiated into the Epsilon Lambda Chapter of Alpha Kappa Alpha Sorority, Inc at the University of Houston.

Aretha Franklin- The late Queen of Soul is also an honorary member of Delta Sigma Theta sorority, Inc.

Nikki Giovanni- Poet and writer is a proud member of Delta Sigma Theta sorority, Inc.

Lena Horne- The legendary singer/actress was also a proud member of Delta Sigma Theta, Inc.

Anna Maria Horsford- Anna Maria is a proud member of Sigma Gamma Rho sorority, Inc.

Cathy Hughes- Founder of Radio One and TV One, Cathy Hughes is a proud member of Alpha Kappa Alpha Sorority, Inc.

Zora Neale Hurston- Zora was initiated into the Zeta Phi Beta Sorority at Howard University.

Syleena Johnson- Syleena is a proud member of Zeta Phi Beta, Inc.

Star Jones- Star is a proud member of the Alpha Kappa Alpha, Inc.

Alicia Keys- Alicia became an honorary member of the historic Alpha Kappa Alpha Sorority in 2004.

Coretta Scott King- The First Lady of the Civil Rights Movement Coretta Scott King was the model Alpha Kappa Alpha because of her tireless community service.

Brandy Norwood- Brandy is a proud member of Alpha Kappa Alpha, Inc.

K. Michelle- K. Michelle pledged Delta Sigma Theta while attending Florida A&M.

Lana "MC Lyte" Moore- Female rap legend and co-founder of the Hip Hop Sisters Foundation "MC Lyte" is a proud member of Sigma Gamma Rho Sorority, Inc.

Toni Morrison- The Pulitzer Prize winning author is a proud member of Alpha Kappa Alpha Sorority, Inc.

Soledad O'Brien- Soledad is a proud member of Delta Sigma Theta Sorority, Inc.

Holly Robinson Peete- Holly is a proud member of Alpha Kappa Alpha, Inc.

L. Marion Poe- First Black Woman admitted to the bar, Southern U.S. is a member of Sigma Gamma Rho Sorority, Inc.

Kelly Price- Kelly became an honorary member of Sigma Gamma Rho sorority in 2006.

Keisha Knight Pulliam- This former "Cosby" kid joined the Delta Sigma Theta sorority while attending Spelman College.

Phylicia Rashad- Phylicia became a member of the Alpha chapter of Alpha Kappa Alpha Sorority, Inc., while attending Howard University.

Victoria Rowell- Victoria is a proud member of the Sigma Gamma Rho sorority, Inc.

Wilma Rudolph- Olympic Track Star is a proud member of Delta Sigma Theta Sorority, Inc.

Jada Pinkett Smith- Jada is a proud member of the Alpha Kappa Alpha Sorority, Inc.

Ebony Steele- Steele is a proud member of Delta Sigma Theta, Inc.

Sheryl Underwood- Sheryl is not only a member, she's a former president of Zeta Phi Beta Sorority, Inc.

Joyce Williams Warren- First Black Arkansas Judge is a proud member of Sigma Gamma Rho, Inc.

Dionne Warwick- Dionne is a honorary member of Zeta Phi Beta Sorority, Inc.

Ruth Whitehead Whaley- First Black Woman in U.S. to practice law is a proud member of Sigma Gamma Rho, Inc.

Kym Whitley- Kym is a proud member of Delta Sigma Theta, Inc.

Dr. Deborah Wolfe- The late Former U.S. Education Chief was a proud member of Zeta Phi Beta, Inc.

Resources

Below are additional resources for you to research many of the topics discussed to give you a stronger foundation as you apply them to your goals. There are many other resources out there so take the initiative to do your part to move forward. Think about what options you have as you learn to explore new possibilities.

Education

The College Board: www.collegeboard.org

The College Navigator: www.nces.ed.gov

Cappex: www.cappex.com

College Majors: www.collegemajors101.com

College Insight: www.college-insight.org

College Results: www.collegeresults.org

Mentorship

Mentoring USA: www.mentorihgusa.org

Big Brothers Big Sisters of America:

Self-Empowerment

Boys and Girls Club of America: www.bgca.org Empowering Black Men and Boys to Transform Their Communities: www.okprogram.org

Black Girls Rock: http://www.blackgirlsrockinc.com

Money

https://www.mindmoneymedia.com/

The US Mint: www.themint.org

Balance Track: www.balancetrack.org

Warren Buffett Advice: http://www.cnbc. com/2013/11/22/buffett-how-to-teach-your-your- kids-about-moneycommentary.html

Teen Entrepreneurs

http://www.teenbusiness.com/ http://www.inc.com/ss/6-richest-teen-entrepreneurs http://www.cnn.com/2014/12/08/business/teen-entrepreneurs-making-millions/

https://www.entrepreneur.com/topic/kids Business Plans: SBA.gov

Girl Power

PowerPlay NYC: https://www.powerplaynyc.org/stars-citywide-girls-initiative

Gyrl Wonder: https://www.gyrlwonder.org

Pay It Forward

Volunteering: www.volunteermatch.org Do Something: www.dosomething.org/us

http://www.themint.org/teens/saving-tricks.html

How Teens Can Become Millionaires

https://www.daveramsey.com/blog/how-teens-can-become-millionaires

Anxiety and Depression

The Anxiety and Depression Association of America (ADAA) is an international nonprofit membership organization (with more than 1,800 professional mental health members) and a leader in education, training, and research for anxiety, depression and related disorders. More than 25 million people from around the world visit the ADAA website annually to find current treatment and research information and to access free resources and support. https://adaa.org

Mental Health America (MHA) - founded in 1909 - is the nation's leading community-based nonprofit dedicated to addressing the needs of those living with mental illness and to promoting the overall mental health of all Americans.

http://www.mentalhealthamerica.net/conditions/anxiety-disorders

Contact Me:

www.especially4mepublishing.com

Email:

dr.rouse@especially4mepublishing.com

dr.angeliserouse@yahoo.com

Also From Dr. Rouse

Available wherever books are sold

For more information log on to

www.especially4mepublishing.com